Frederick A. Petersen

Military Review of the Campaign in Virginia and Maryland

Frederick A. Petersen

Military Review of the Campaign in Virginia and Maryland

ISBN/EAN: 9783337813819

Printed in Europe, USA, Canada, Australia, Japan

Cover: Foto ©ninafisch / pixelio.de

More available books at **www.hansebooks.com**

MILITARY REVIEW

OF THE

Campaign in Virginia & Maryland,

UNDER

Generals John C. Fremont, N. P. Banks, Irwin McDowell, Franz Sigel, John Pope, James S. Wadsworth, Wm. H. Halleck and George B. McClellan.

IN

1862,

BY

FRED'K A. PETERSEN.

> *He that is truly dedicated to war*
> *Hath no self-love; nor he that loves himself*
> *Hath not essentially, but by circumstances,*
> *The name of valor.*
> SHAKSPERE.

A Contribution to the Future History of the United States.

NEW-YORK:

WHOLESALE AGENTS: { SINCLAIR TOUSEY, 121 NASSAU STREET, H. DEXTER, 113 NASSAU STREET.

PRICE 15 CENTS.

Entered according to Act of Congress in the year 1862, by F. A. PETERSEN, in the Clerk's Office of the District Court of the Southern District of New-York.

MILITARY REVIEW

OF THE
CAMPAIGN IN VIRGINIA & MARYLAND

In 1862.

On the 12th day of March, 1862, the following orders were published in the City of Washington:

War Gazette Official.

The President's General War Order *No.* 1.

Executive Mansion, Washington, January 27, 1862.

Ordered, That the 22d of February, 1862, be the day for a general movement of the land and naval forces of the United States against the insurgent forces; that especially the army at and about Fortress Monroe, the army of the Potomac, the army of Western Virginia, the army near Munfordsville, Ky., the flotilla at Cairo, and a naval force in the Gulf of Mexico, be ready for a movement on that day.

That all the other forces, both landed and naval, with their respective commanders, obey existing orders for the time, and be ready to obey additional orders when duly given.

That the heads of departments, and especially the Secretaries of War and the Navy, with all their subordinates, and the General-in-Chief, with all other commanders and subordinates of the landed and naval forces, will severally be held to their strict and full responsibilties for the prompt execution of this order.

ABRAHAM LINCOLN.

The President's General War Order *No.* 2.

Executive Mansion, Washington, March 8th, 1862.

Ordered, That the Major-General commanding the Army of the Potomac proceed forthwith to organize that part of the said army destined to enter upon active operations, including the reserve, but excluding the troops to be left in the fortifications about Washington, into four army corps, to be commanded according to seniority of rank, as follows:

" The first corps, consisting of four divisions, by Major-General I. McDowell; the second corps, consisting of three divisions, by Brigadier-General Sumner; the third corps, consisting of three divisions, by Brigadier-General Heintzelman; the fourth corps, consisting of three divisions, by Brigadier-General Keyes.

2d. That the divisions now commanded by the respective Generals form part of their respective corps.

3d. That the forces left for the defence of Washington will be placed in command of Brigadier-General James S. Wadsworth, who shall also be Military Governor of the District of Columbia.

4th. That this order be executed with such promptness and dispatch as not to delay the commencement of the operations already directed to be undertaken by the Army of the Potomac.

5th. The fifth army corps to be commanded by Major-General N. P. Banks, will be formed from his own and General Shields' (late General Lander's) divisions.

ABRAHAM LINCOLN.

The President's War Order No. 3.

Executive Mansion, Washington, March 11th, 1862.

Major-General McClellan having personally taken the field at the head of the Army of the Potomac, until otherwise ordered, is relieved from the command of the other military departments, he maintaining command of the Department of the Potomac. Ordered, further, that the departments now under the respective commands of Generals Halleck and Hunter, together with so much of that under General Buell as lies west of a north and south line drawn through Knoxville, Tenn., be consolidated, and designated the Department of the Mississippi, and that, until otherwise ordered, Major-General Halleck have command of said department. Ordered, also, that the country west of the Department of the Potomac, and east of the Department of the Mississippi, be a military department to be called the Mountain Department, and that the same be commanded by Major-General Fremont. That all the commanders of Departments, after the receipt of this order by them respectively, report severally and directly to the Secretary of War, and that prompt, full, and frequent reports will be expected of all and each of them.

ABRAHAM LINCOLN.

In issuing the General War Orders above reprinted, the President for the first time exercised, in person, the authority as Commander-in-Chief of the army and navy of the United States—an authority which, as far as the army is concerned, he had to the last day of October, 1861, delegated to General Winfield Scott, and since the first day of November, 1861, to General George B. McClellan, of whom, in his Message to Congress, December 3d, 1861, he says: "With

"the retirement of Gen Scott came the executive duty of appointing
"in his stead a General-in-Chief for the army. It is a fortunate cir-
"cumstance that neither in council nor country was there, so far as I
"know, any difference of opinion as to the proper person to be se-
"lected. The retiring chief repeatedly expressed his opinion in
"favor of General McClellan for the position, and in this the nation
"seemed to give an unanimous concurrence. The designation of Gene-
"ral McClellan is, therefore, in a considerable degree, the selection of
"the country as well as of the executive, and hence there is better rea-
"son to hope there will be given him the confidence and cordial support,
"thus by fair implication promised, and without which he cannot,
"with so full efficiency, save the country."

What reason had the President to interfere personally with the affairs of the army, when General McClellan continued to be General-in-Chief, and had been especially charged with the entire command of the army? It cannot be want of confidence in General McClellan's capacity or loyalty, because Order No. 1 leaves General McClellan in command of the entire army more than six weeks after it had been executed; and the President could not possibly leave a man, whom he has reason to doubt, in so important a position. It cannot be the imperative necessity of issuing an order to the army which precluded the loss of time necessary for its communication to the General-in-Chief, because Order No. 1, in a military point of view, orders very little, if anything, except *that January 22d, 1862, be the day for a general movement against the insurgent forces*, and even this it modifies at once, by stating that certain six different armies (that is, the entire army) shall be *ready for* a movement on that day; it next orders that the forces shall *obey existing* orders for the time, and *be ready* to obey *additional* orders when *duly given;* a fundamental principle in all military organizations, for the express republication of which, in so unusual a form, there does not seem to exist any necessity whatever; finally, the order informs the Secretaries of War and of the Navy, the Commander-in-Chief, and all other commanders and subordinates, that they will be held to strict and full responsibilities for the prompt execution of the order, which, of course, does not burden them with any new responsibility. It cannot be that the President had changed his views as to the practicability and correctness of the plan of the campaign for 1862, as laid out by Gen. McClellan, because the order does not indicate the least change in the said plan; McClellan proceeded in its execution, and the President allows six weeks to pass by, before he publishes his orders, and therefore, McClellan's plan is adhered to six weeks longer; besides this, the President professes to adhere to it, wherever opportunity offers to express his opinion. It cannot be that the President thinks General McClellan less prompt, precise, or expeditious in the issuing of orders for a movement than himself; because order No. 2 proves in its first three specifications that an important part of the organization of the Army of the Potomac, (that is, its formation in army corps, upon which the efficacy of that army seems materially to depend, as well as the organization of a sufficient force for the security, and, in case of need, for the defence of the works around Washington,) had been entirely overlooked in War Order No. 1; while specification 4 shows that no operations of the Army of the Potomac as yet had been undertaken, and that consequently, as far as the last named army is concerned, said Order No. 1 had been issued prematurely, and therefore had better not been issued at all. It cannot possibly be that the President had differed with General McClellan as to the *proper time when, the co-operative execution of the latter's plan* for the campaign *ought to be commenced*, and that the President, overruling McClellan's advice, had issued Order No. 1; because the long delay between the date of the order and its publication, would go far to show that the President had become convinced, that he had issued it *long before the proper time*. While War Orders No. 1 and 2 do not seem to throw any light upon the reason for which they were issued, the following letter, early in March published in and directed to the editor of the New York Tribune, by Mr. Edwin M. Stanton, may perhaps lead us in the proper direction:

SIR: I cannot suffer undue merit to be ascribed to my official action. The glory of our recent victories belongs to the gallant officers that fought the battles. No share of it belongs to me.

Much has recently been said of military combination and organizing victory. I hear such phrases with apprehension. They commenced in infidel France with the Italian campaign, and resulted in Waterloo. Who can organize victory? Who can combine the elements of success on the battle field? We owe our recent victories to the spirit of the Lord, that moved our soldiers to dash into battle and filled the hearts of our enemies with terror and dismay. The inspiration that conquered in battle was in the hearts of the soldiers and from on high; and wherever there is the same inspiration there will be the same results. Patriotic spirit with resolute courage in officers and men is a military combination that never failed.

We may well rejoice at the recent victories, for they teach us that battles are to be won now and by us in the same and only manner

that they were ever won by any people or in any age since the days of Joshua, by boldly pursuing and striking the foe. What, under the blessing of Providence, I conceive to be the true organization of victory and military combination to end this war, was declared in a few words by General Grant's message to General Buckner: " I propose to move immediately on your works."
Yours truly,
EDWIN M. STANTON.

Mr. Stanton was appointed Secretary of War about the middle of January. A controversy between the daily Press of the various political parties, as to what General had laid out the plan of the campaign, in the execution of which, Burnside in North Carolina, Dupont in South Carolina, and Generals Grant, Buell and Thomas in Kentucky and in Tennessee, had gained advantages over the rebels; in which controversy Mr. Edwin M. Stanton's name was also mentioned as the originator of the said plan, at a time when he, a lawyer of high standing, was deeply engaged in his profession. In consequence of this allusion to his merit in the matter, the Secretary of War wrote the above letter to the editor in whose paper the allusion had been made. However much he may try to conceal it by infidel France, by the spirit of the Lord, by inspiration, by patriotic spirit, by Joshua, and by the blessing of Providence, it is nevertheless clear, that Mr. Stanton's letter is nothing more nor less than one continuous slur, at military science and military leaders in general, on Napoleon Bonaparte, the most brilliant of them, and at General McClellan in particular. He had made the plan for the campaign of 1862, and had repeatedly declared, that he could and would not order a general movement until *all* the necessary preliminary combinations would have been completed. Let us see how far Mr. Stanton's apprehension, with which he hears the phrase of *military combination* and *organizing victory* is well-founded, and how far his argument against those phrases is correct, by investigating events which had taken place only a short time before Mr. Stanton became Secretary of War, and which therefore ought to have been fresh in his memory, when he wrote the letter in question. At the battle of Belmont, November 1861, where General Ulysses S. Grant, (whose spirited message to General Buckner, the Secretary of War conceives to declare *the true organization of victory and military combination*,) had supreme command, our soldiers rushed to battle and filled the hearts of the enemy with terror and dismay, but only till the superior military combinations of the rebel generals could be brought to bear upon General Grant's forces; when for the very want of a *proper organization to secure victory,* he had to retreat from the enemy's camp, which at the first rush of his gallant men, he had actually occupied. Not having exercised strategical wisdom and experience to protect his line of retreat and his point of embarkation, he suffered fearfully, and re-embarked only a small portion of his terribly cut-up corps. General Grant, and General McClernand under him, tried to do his duty to the best of his understanding at the time ; but he lacked experience, did not completely mature his operations before he commenced its execution, and consequently failed and was badly defeated. His more perfect combinations at a later period proved how he profited by the lesson received at Belmont. Does Mr. Stanton mean to say that *the spirit of the Lord* who inspired General Grant's soldiers to rush into battle at Belmont, made right about face, when they had entered the rebel camp, and then went and inspired the rebels to rush upon our brave fellows, and kill them and drive them into the river ? or that General Grant and his brave troops had lost *their patriotic spirit, and resolute courage* when they had fought their way into the enemy's camp ? Or, that the *inspiration from high,* entered first the hearts of General Grant's army, and then slipt out and went into the hearts of the rebels ? Or, that the *spirit of the Lord,* in consideration that both of them had been very naughty, directed that by the *blessing of Providence,* first the soldiers of the Confederate States, and then those of the United States of America, should receive a sound thrashing ? We know him to be too good a lawyer, if not Secretary of War, to believe in any such blasphemous nonsense. We for our part, firmly believe that the Almighty will bless our good cause and give us the victory in the end ; but we expect this gift precisely in the same manner as he gives us our daily bread ; that is after we have made all reasonable exertions to earn it ourselves. To win battles, we must understand to make military combinations *to gain,* and proper provisions *to secure victory,* otherwise we will see many repetitions of the affair at Belmont, because the greatest captain of modern history, truly said : " In war, Providence is generally with the heaviest artillery." That is with artillery placed in the best position. Mr. Stanton forgets what he has read, or ought to have read, long before he became Secretary of War, in Greek and Latin, about the military combinations of Xenophon, of Xerxes, of Caesar, of Hannibal, and others ; when he says, these *phrases* commenced in infidel France, with the Italian campaign, and ended with Waterloo. Aside of this historical incorrectness, how does the history of the

French wars, during the time fixed by the Secretary of War, justify him in hearing "these phrases with apprehension?"

The corruption prevailing at the court of the elder Bourbons had, during about twenty years next previous to the time to which Mr. Stanton alludes, been more or less systematically infused into the aristocracy, and through them, into the French army, where the scions of nobility controlled the highest commissions; (because a corrupt commander is sure to corrupt his entire command in an astonishingly short time). The study and practice of military science was subsequently more and more neglected, and the French army became, in the same proportion, despised by other military nations, in particular by the German powers, who, thanks to the military genius of Frederick the Great, of Prussia, and to the lessons a-la-Belmont, in military combinations, and in perfect military organization which he had given to the various leading generals of Maria Theresa, of Austria. They possessed well officered and perfectly disciplined armies, which, at the instigation, and with the pecuniary aid of England, that had no organized army, they boldly sent to the French frontiers, with the intention of upholding or reinstating the rotten dynasty of the banished royal family. The French armies were defeated almost in every engagement, and if it had not been for the deep-rooted hostility of the people in the provinces against the foreign invader, the armies of the coalition, as the German armies were called, would probably have penetrated to the capital of France. But the military genius of Napoleon Bonaparte, perfectly regulated and disciplined by long and profound study of the science of war, led the indignant and aroused masses, by the most sublime military combinations, across the Alps into that Italian campaign,—to which the honorable Secretary of War alludes in his *Tribune* letter,—and on the 12th of April, 1796, at Montenotte, gained his first victory over the Austrian field marshal D'Argenteau. Almost without a single serious reverse, frequently against largely superior forces, led by commanders who had gained great fame as military leaders, (by keeping strictly in the beaten track laid out by those, who had become stationary, when Frederick the Great finished his lesson to them). Many there were then, as there are now, who, although Napoleon had in an almost incredibly short time, driven the Austrian armies out of Italy, declared that nothing but good luck and the courage of the army had caused these victories, and that Napoleon's military strategy and tactics had nothing to do with it. How far this opinion had spread, may be well illustrated by the following historical facts:

Frederick William III., king of Prussia, anticipating the possibility of collisions with the young emperor, early in 1805, called a council of state, for the purpose of deciding upon a policy to be adopted by Prussia in her future relations with France. Several of the oldest generals were in attendance; the king, during the deliberation presented the view whether, in consideration of the unparalleled successes of the young chieftain against the best Austrian generals, which seemed to indicate an entirely new strategy on his part, it might not, after all, be the wisest policy to try to come to a peaceful understanding, or, perhaps, to an alliance with him? When general Von Branchitsch, a man high in rank by long service, twisting his moustache, replied, "He had the honor of assuring his majesty, upon his honor, that in the Prussian army there were at least five or six such Napoleon Bonapartes." Upon this assurance, the king decided to side with Austria against Napoleon, which decision led to the battle of Jena, October 17, 1806, where the Prussian army was completely routed, before the commanders were fully aware that they had been attacked; and to the peace of Tilsit, July 7th and 9th, 1807, where, by the grace of Napoleon, Frederick William III., retained a very small portion of his kingdom. These same military combinations, commencing in Italy in 1796, carried Napoleon and his French armies, in fifteen years, almost without any reverses, victorious from Italy through Holland, Belgium, and all the German sovereignties, without a single exception, to the western frontiers of the Russian empire, which they reached in October, 1812.* So that if military combinations are properly applied by the generals at the head of our armies, they will operate in a similar manner as they did in the case referred to in Mr. Stanton's letter. The rebellion will, by their application, be crushed in a comparatively very short time. Mr. Stanton's reason for his apprehension, in hearing the phrase alluded to, are, therefore, not better than his explanation of the real causes *to which we owe our recent victories.*

When, after having thus glanced at Mr. Stanton's *Tribune* letter, we read the President's War Order, No. 3, we find that this order:

---

* It would exceed the limits of this essay to analyze the reasons which caused the destruction of Napoleon's army in Russia, his defeats in 1813 and 1814, and his final overthrow, June 18, 1815. But it is certain, beyond all doubt, that neglect of complete combinations, and well organized victories on his side, and the adoption of Napoleon's principles to the most complete combinations and organizations by his opponents, were among the most effective agencies to bring about that result.

1st. Relieves General McClellan of his command as general-in-chief of the armies of the United States, and assigns him the command of *the Department of the Potomac.*

2d. That it consolidates the commands under Generals Halleck, Hunter, and a portion of that under General Buell, in the Department of the Mississippi, under General Halleck.

3d. That it relieves Generals Hunter and Buell of the commands of departments.

4th. That it creates a new department, bound east by the department of the Potomac, and west by the department of the Mississippi, to be called the *Mountain Department.*

5th. That it reinstates in to a command General John C. Fremont, who had been deprived of his command in October, 1861.

6th. That it gives General Fremont command of the new Mountain Department.

7th. That it orders the commanders of all the departments to report severally and direct to *the Secretary of War,* and consequently gives to Mr. Edwin M. Stanton, in addition to his office as Secretary of War, that of *de facto* General-in-Chief of the Armies of the United States.

Order No. 3, therefore, makes up in importance of its contents, what Orders No. 1 and No. 2 seem to be void of; and it goes far to confirm our opinion that, because all these important changes in the organization and the command of the army, were considered necessary for its efficiency against the enemy, the President's War Order No. 1, was issued decidedly before the proper time. But even the material changes in its organization, produced by order No. 3, do not seem to have given to the army the desired efficiency to crush the rebellion in the shortest possible time. Mr. Stanton's desire for executive employment seems still to have exceeded the enormous responsibilities already assumed; because, early in April, 1862, the President directs two more military departments to be created, one of them to embrace that portion of Virginia and Maryland lying between the Mountain Department and the Blue Ridge, to be called the *Department of the Shenandoah;* the other to be designated the Department of the *Rappahanock,* and to comprise the portion of Virginia east of the Blue Ridge, and West of the Potomac and the Fredericksburg and Richmond Railroad, including the District of Columbia and the Patuxent. General McDowell is placed in command of the latter, and General Banks of the former Department. This operation for improving the efficiency of the army, it will be seen, deprives General

McClellan of two army corps belonging to the Army of the Potomac, besides of a good slice of the Department of the Potomac; and it adds to the corps under General McDowell, (already the largest of any in the Army of the Potomac, by the President's War Order No. 2) the entire force, by that same order, placed under command of Brig. General James S. Wadsworth, to protect the works around the City of Washington.

All these changes in the army and reductions in the extent of Gen. McClellan's official province, it must be remembered, were made at a time when, under that general's chief command, a succession of Union victories had been achieved; by Burnside, at Roanoke Island; by Thomas and Schoepf, at Somerset and Bowling Green; by Grant, at Fort Henry and Donelson; and by Lander, in Western Virginia. If there could be a possibility for a lasting advantage to the instigator, we would be strongly tempted to the belief that all the above noted peculiar changes in the organization and command of the army, were made in strict compliance with the old adage *divide et impera.*

Considering Mr. Stanton's Tribune letter, in which, as we have seen, without regard to historical truth, and in violation of sound common sense, he tries to criticise and depreciate the strategical principles of the General-in-Chief, and consequently to undermine his influence with the army. Considering that by every one of these charges McClellan's command and official influence is reduced, while the official importance of Mr. Edwin M. Stanton is extended, and his direct control over the army increased, it does not seem likely, although Abraham Lincoln is to the country responsible for all these peculiar remodelings of the army, that there could be found in all New England a single Yankee who would not guess that Mr. Stanton is the real instigator of all these mischievous intermeddlings. This then is the manner in which the confidence and cordial support—by the President in his message, Dec. 3, '61, delared, *by fair implication promised, and without which he can not with so full efficiency serve the country*—were given to General McClellan by those highest in the country's offices.

The organization of an army and the character of the commanders of army corps, constitute in time of war the most influential agencies for the co-operation of the several corps and the success of the army. Let us inquire what military or other achievements have secured to the respective Generals placed in command of the various army corps in Virginia, the distinction of being by the President's War Order, entrusted with commissions, of so great influonce in the speedy or slow termination of this expensive and terrible war, therefore of vast importance to the country, and of enormous responsibility to the Generals themselves ? Commencing on the right wing, we find John C. Fremont, Major General United States Army, in command of the *Mountain Department.* General Fremont had served in the Army of the United States prior to the acquisition of the State of California ; he had explored the country west of the Mississippi, and had, at the head of a small command, penetrated as far as California ; this expedition, although not made against an enemy, caused the gallant leader some trouble, placed him in a false position towards his superior officers, caused him to be court-martialled, and finally to resign his commission in the army. On the other hand it secured to him a landed estate of, according to general opinion, regal extent, and of immense value, known as the Mariposa Grant, the title of which, although long disputed, has finally been adjudicated to the General. In a military point of view, this exploration was of no significance, certainly not as in any possible manner indicating qualifications for a command of large force.*

Having attended to his California estates for several years, John C· Fremont returned to New York, and was nominated by his political friends for the office of President of the United States, and thereby became widely known all over the Union. He was not elected, and was, four years later, when the Republican party again had to select a nominee, dropped by them to make room for Abraham Lincoln. The outbreak of the rebellion found Mr. Fremont in Europe; he at once exerted his influence in favor of the North, secured and sent to Wash-

---

* To show what can be done with a few men. We quote from a pamphlet entitled "Fremont and McClellan, Yonkers, New York," where, at page 7, the military achievements of General Fremont, are thus summed up : " Fremont with twenty-five men, had crossed the great mountains and deserts of America, amid untold hardships, yet with signal success ; subsisting his horses on the bark of trees, and his men upon the flesh of horses, and had, with this force, recruited by a few Americans resident in California, while still unaware of the existence of war with Mexico, hoisted the Bear Flag of California independence, prevented the British fleet from seizing this province, driven out the Mexican forces, and when he learned of the existence of our war with Mexico, exchanged the Bear Flag for the Stars and Stripes ; thus giving to his country, as a province, California, the land whose rivers ran over glistening sands of gold. As a soldier, it was his good fortune to win to his country a province whose untold wealth repaid the cost incurred by Taylor and Scott in conquering territory to be afterwards surrendered."

ington a splendid battery of rifled cannon, with large quantities of other arms, and returned with his family to his native land. Before his arrival, the President appointed him Major General of the United States Army, a rank at that time held only by General McClellan. When General Fremont reached Washington, he was placed in command of the Department of the West, headquarters St. Louis, and entered upon his duties in the early part of August, 1861.

Before the troops under General Fremont had made a movement *en masse*,* Colonel Blair of Missouri, a leader of the so-called Republican party, presented serious charges against General Fremont—was put under and kept in arrest by the General for some time, and was then restored to his command without any sort of trial, and without having retracted any of his charges. The importance thereof caused General Thomas, Adjutant General of the army of the United States under General Scott, to be sent to the headquarters of General Fremont for the purpose of investigating the charges preferred by Colonel Blair. The report of General Thomas to the Commander-in-Chief of our armies, bore out Colonel Blair's charges. President Lincoln, deprived General Fremont of his command without trial or court-martial, October 20th, 1861.† To military men it was and is to this day a matter of surprise and deep regret that General Fremont lacked, to say the least, the respect due to the army of the United States, wherein he holds a high commission, the proper self-respect and *esprit du corps*, to demand a court-martial.

The charges of Colonel Blair and those of General Thomas had never been retracted. General Fremont had not sought an opportunity to prove them to be false. The staff officers of General Fremont were almost all dismissed from the army, some of them having insisted upon trial by court-martial, have not been tried yet. General Thomas is still Adjutant General of the army; but four months after he has been deprived of his command, War Order No. 3 places General John C. Fremont in command of a new department.

Measures like this must of necessity operate detrimentally upon the *morale*, the *esprit du corps*, the discipline, and consequently upon the

---

* The two brilliant affairs under General Franz Sigel at Carthage and at Rolla, although they demonstrated the military eminence of that gallant soldier, were participated in only by a very insignificant and detached force.

† The statement on page 18 previously mentioned of the *Crisis* pamphlet, that McClellan is responsible for the removal of Fremont from his command is untrue, because General McClellan did not become General-in-Chief of the Army until November, 1861.

efficiency of the army. The conviction thereof in Europe is so complete that in the present century, in no country except in Turkey, the government would appoint a General to a command whose fair fame was in the least tarnished by any unrepudiated charges. No, General, if so appointed, would accept a command before he had, by the verdict of a court-martial, been fully and honorably cleared of any suspicion of a conduct unbecoming an officer; because every officer is fully aware that accepting a command without having previously demanded and obtained opportunity to reestablish his fair fame, he would make himself a target for every officer in his command.

Immediately after the last Italian war, in which the new strategy and tactics of Louis Napoleon, for the first time astonished the military world, Lieutenant General von Bonin, the Secretary of War to the King of Prussia, presented to the government a plan for the reorganization of the Prussian army; the King, after hearing Bonin's explanations of his plan, in a full Cabinet Council, approved of it, and ordered it to be prepared in form of a bill, to be presented for the approbation of Congress. While General von Bonin was yet engaged in the execution of this order, the King sent for him, and in a private interview, told him he had, on reflection, ordered one of his aids to introduce some merely formal changes in von Bonin's original plan, which he wished him to examine and to adopt in the bill he was preparing. General von Bonin read the amendments and informed his Majesty that he would not in the least object to any merely formal alterations in his original plan, as long as the fundamental principle thereof was adhered to; that the amendment handed to him, by the King, entirely changed the principle upon which his own plan had been based, and that consequently he had to regret the necessity that prevented him to adopt the amendment in his own bill. The King replied that he would consider the matter.

The following day General von Bonin received two letters from the King; the first deprived him of the office of Secretary of War, for disobedience to the orders of the King; the second appointed him Commander-in-Chief of the eighth army corps, on the French frontier, the most important military command in the army. General von Bonin at once replied, that an officer who had been so unfortunate as to deserve to be deprived of his command for disobedience was forever unworthy to hold a command in the Prussian army; he therefore respectfully tendered his resignation as an officer of the army, to take effect immediately. Congress rejected the amended plan for the army reorganization, and at the present moment this same question has caused the second ministerial crisis in Berlin.

Our own army, we very much fear, will never be what the country has a right to expect it to be, before our officers understand to act upon principles similar to those expressed by Lieutenant-General van Bonin. In Turkey this principle has been neglected, in consequence of the universal corruption with which that beautiful country is cursed. Officers charged with malfeasance were deprived of a command to-day, and trusted with another one a few days afterwards; the consequence was that, Marshal Diebitch, the Russian commander-in-chief, in 1829, found that the commander of almost every fortress (however impregnable by nature and artificial fortifications), had his fixed price for which he surrendered; so that the Russian army reached Adrianople, a short distance from Constantinople, before the Sultan considered it possible that the siege of the first frontier fortress could have fairly been commenced. The Turkish High-Admiral when sent with a large fleet against the rebellious Pacha of Egypt, took the entire fleet in to the Egyptian port and surrendered it to the rebel. Since that time the *esprit du corps* in the army of the Sultan has been revived and encouraged in every possible manner; corruption has been punished whenever detected, and the result of this change of sentiment has been demonstrated in the many brilliant affairs performed by the army as well as the navy of the Sultan during the last Crimean war. Omar Pasha has established a fair reputation for the army, and the brilliant fight of a single Turkish vessel against five Russian steamers in the disgraceful affair of Sinope, have gained respect for the "sick man's" navy.

General N. P. Banks, the commander of the Department of the Shenandoah, on the left of General Fremont's department, had distinguished himself as Speaker of the House of Representatives, as Governor of Massachusetts, where he caused a complete reorganization of the militia, which he militarised so far, that at the outbreak of the rebellion, Colonel Butler's Massachusetts regiment was the first in the country on its march to Washington. Declining the re-nomination for Governor, General Banks found in the management of an extensive Railroad system a new field for the display and development of his executive talents. This so much the better qualified him, at the outbreak of the rebellion, to accept a command of a Division in the army of the Potomac. By earnest study, by strict military conduct, by the rapid promotion of the efficiency of his men, by the well-conceived disposition of his forces, to guard the line of the upper Potomac, and by his successful occupation of Harper's Ferry, he had proved his adaptedness for a military command on a larger scale, and had received the appointment as Major-General of Volunteers. On the left of General Banks' department joined the department of the Rappahannock, under Major-General I. McDowell.

General McDowell at the commencement of the rebellion held a commission as Major in the United States army, was very soon called to Washington, promoted to a Brigadier-Generalship, and entrusted with the chief command of an army in and around Washington in June, 1861. This army went under his command into what is known as the first battle of Bull Run; General McDowell came out of it and made the following official report:

HEADQUARTERS, DEPARTMENT NORTH-EASTERN VIRGINIA,
ARLINGTON, Va., August 4, 1861.

Lieutenant-Colonel E. D. TOWNSEND, Assistant Adjutant-General,
Headquarters of the Army, Washington, D. C.

COLONEL—I have the honor to submit the following report of the battle of the 21st of July, near Manassas, Virginia. It has been delayed till this time from the inability of the subordinate commanders to get earlier a true account of the state of their commands.

* * * * *

The divisions were ordered to march at half-past two o'clock A.M., so as to arrive on the ground early in the day, and thus avoid the heat which is to be expected at this season. There was delay in the first division getting out of its camp on the road, and the other divisions were in consequence between two and three hours behind the time appointed—a great misfortune, as events turned out.

* * * * *

Inasmuch as General McDowell had never before held a command, a military reading of his report will afford the fairest basis for an opinion regarding his qualification and merits as a commander of an army.

The report shows everywhere the General's endeavor to report the facts as they actually occurred, and to neither conceal nor to magnify anything.

After having given a description of the proceedings during the 21st day of July which, (after only a portion of his army had seen the enemy, or had been engaged, he says,) resulted in a hasty retreat, acomplete rout, and finally in an irresistable panic; carrying everything in one promiscuous mass of men and beast before it, and some of the disorganised troops by way of Washington as far as New York; and after having claimed credit for distinguished conduct for a great many officers of the various corps and of his staff, he proceeds:

As my position may warrant, even if it does not call for some explanation of the causes, as far as they can be seen, which led to the results herein stated, I trust it may not be out of place if I refer in a few words to the immediate antecedents of the battle. When I submitted to the General-in-Chief, in compliance with his verbal instructions, the plan of operations and estimate of force required, the time I was to proceed to carry it into effect was fixed for the 8th July, Monday. Every facility possible was given me by the General-in-Chief and heads of the administrative departments in making the necessary preparations. But the regiments, owing, I was told, to want of transportation, came over slowly. Many of them did not come across till eight or nine days after the time fixed upon, and went forward without my even seeing them, and without having been together before in a brigade. The sending reinforcements to General Patterson, by drawing off the wagons, was a further and unavoidable cause of delay. Notwithstanding the herculean efforts of the Quartermaster General, and his favoring me in every way, the wagons for ammunition, subsistence, &c., and the horses for the trains and the artillery, did not all arrive for more than a week after the time appointed to move. I was not even prepared as late as the 15th ultimo, and the desire I should move became great, and it was wished I should not, if possible, delay longer than Tuesday, the 16th ultimo, When I did set out, on the 16th, I was still deficient in wagons for subsistence. But I went forward, trusting to their being procured in time to follow me. The trains thus hurriedly gathered together, with horses, wagons, drivers, and wagon managers, all new and unused to each other, moved with difficulty and disorder, and was the cause of a day's delay in getting the provisions forward, making it necessary to make on Sunday the attack we should have made on Saturday. I could not, with every exertion, get forward with the troops earlier than we did. I wished to go to Centreville the second day, which would have taken us there on the 17th, and enabled us, so far as they were concerned, to go into action on the 19th, instead of the 21st, but when I went forward from Fairfax Court House beyond Germantown, to urge them forward, I was told it was impossible for the men to march further. They had only come from Vienna, about six miles, and it was not more than six and a half miles further to Centreville—in all a march of twelve and a half miles; but the men were foot-weary, not so much, I was told, by the distance marched, as by the time they had been on foot, caused by the obstructions in the road, and the slow pace we had to move to avoid ambuscades. The men were, moreover, unaccustomed to marching, their bodies not in condition for that kind of work, and not used to carrying even the load of light marching order. We crossed Bull Run with about 18,000 men of all arms, the fifth division (Miles and Richardson's brigade) on the left, at Blackburn's Ford to Centreville, and Schenck's brigade, of Tyler's division, on the left of the road, near the stone bridge, not participating in the main action. The numbers opposed to us have been variously estimated. I may safely say, and avoid even the appearance of exaggeration, that the enemy brought up all he could which were not kept engaged elsewhere. He had notice of our coming on the 17th, and had from that time until the 21st to bring up whatever he had. It is known that in estimating the force to go against Manassas, I engaged not to have to do with the enemy's forces under Johnson, then kept in check in the valley by Major General Patterson, or those kept engaged by Major General Butler, and I know every offort was made by the General-in-Chief that this should be done, and that even if Johnson joined Beauregard, it would not be because he could be followed by General Patterson, but from causes not necessary for me to refer to, if I knew them at all. This was not done, and the enemy was free to assemble from every direction in numbers only limited by the amount of this railroad rolling stock and his supply of provisions. To the forces, therefore, we drove in from Fairfax Court House, Fairfax Station, Germantown, and Centreville, and those under Beauregard at Manassas, must be added those under Johnston from Winchester, and those brought up by Davis from Richmond and other places at the South, to which is to be added the levy *en masse* ordered by the Richmond authorities, which was ordered to assemble at Manassas. What all this amounted to I cannot say—certainly much more than we attacked them with. I could not, as I have said more early, push on faster, nor could I delay. A large and the best part of my forces were three months' volunteers, whose term of service was about to expire, but who were sent forward as having long enough to serve for the purpose of the exhibition. On the eve of the battle, the Fourth Pennsylvania regiment of volunteers and the battery of volunteer artillery of the New York Eighth militia, whose term of service expired, insisted on their discharge. I wrote to the regiment, expressing a request for them to remain a short time, and the Hon. Secretary of War, who was at the time on the ground, tried to induce the battery to remain at least five days. But in vain. They insisted on their discharge that night. It was granted, and the next morning, when the army moved forward into battle, these troops moved to the rear to the sound of the enemy's cannon. In the next few days, day by day, I should have lost ten thousand of the best armed, drilled, officered, and disciplined troops in the army. In other words, every day which added to the strength of the enemy made us weaker. In conclusion, I desire to say, in reference to the events of the 21st ult., that the general order for the battle to which I referred was, with slight modifications, literally conformed to; that the corps were brought over Bull Run in the manner proposed, and put into action as before arranged, and that up to late in the afternoon every movement ordered was carrying us successfully to the object we had proposed before starting—that of getting to the railroad leading from Manassas to the valley of Virginia, and going on it far enough to break up and destroy the communication and interviens between the forces under Beauregard and those under Johnston. And could we have fought a day or a few hours sooner, there is everything to show how we could have continued successful, even against the odds with which we contended. I have the honor to be, very respectfully, your most obedient servant,

IRWIN McDOWELL,
Brigadier-General Commanding.

We see that, twelve days before the 21st of August, General McDowell intended to move; that, as he says, notwithstanding the greatest efforts of, and all possible facilities given him by the commander-in-chief, and the heads of the departments, the regiments did not come in till eight or nine days later. What a horrible state must the organization of the army have been in, if the combined exertions of all these high personages, to acknowledge which the general twice takes occasion, could not provide better results than this utter failure in everything? Who was to blame that the regiments went forward without the general having seen them; and without having been together before in a brigade? Certainly nobody but General McDowell himself. The regiments could not come to look for or to see the general, but it was his business and his most important duty to go and see them, to get acquainted with them, and make himself known to them; to order them to be brigaded; to designate the several regiments for every brigade, and to order what brigade drill they should become accustomed to. If he was not even prepared on the fifteenth of May to move, what had he, as a soldier, to do with a *desire* and a *wish* that *he should not delay beyond the sixteenth*? And how could he think of ever justifying himself for having moved against an enemy, before being in every respect completely prepared and ready? As a general, responsible for the lives and safety of every man in his command, and as a soldier, he has to receive and to give *orders;* with *desires* and *wishes* he has nothing whatever to do; but in particular has he not to jeopardise the lives of the men entrusted to him. Even, when on the 17th day of July, he joined his troops on the march, and found them foot-sore and unprepared for a campaign, he did not see the folly, nay crime, he was committing, in seeking an engagement with an enemy, without the most absolute necessity. The reasons given why he could not delay any longer, are the most powerful reasons that should have induced him not to seek an engagement at all. If, as he says, by the expiration of the term of service of a large proportion of his men, his army would day by day have been reduced and become weaker; he, and every military man, ought to have foreseen that a defeat in battle (and he had, according to his own statement of facts, nothing else to expect), would deprive him and the country of the entire army, and place the capitol and the Government at the mercy of the enemy. Still more unwarrantable appears the forward movement in the face, first of the distinct declaration of Colonel Burnside, of Rhode Island, that in the presence of senator Wilson, of Massachusetts, he told General McDowell, two days before the battle, that the army was not prepared, and ought not to move forward to an engagement; to which McDowell replied, *that if he could not fight now, he could not fight in six months*, because his *best men would go home;* when Burnside said, better fight not at all than fight with his army in its present condition, which remark produced on senator Wilson's face an expression indicating that he thought the colonel to be a coward; *second*, in consideration of the small and insignificant purpose for which the existence of the then entire army of the country was put in jeopardy, to wit, *to break up by destruction of the railroad, the communication between two corps of the enemy.* For the last six weeks, these had both been kept in check and harmless, by the presence of the United States troops, respectively, under General Patterson, on the upper Potomac, and near Washington, under McDowell, and could have been kept in check a great while longer. *This, General McDowell himself, designates the object of the movement,* both at the commencement and towards the end of his report. If the entire army had followed the example of the fourth Pennsylvania volunteers, and of the artillery of the eighth New York militia, the disgrace of July 21st, would probably have been avoided.

Finding General McDowell entirely wanting in the fundamental principles of military foresight, and organizing qualities, as well as in a due consideration of his responsibilities and duties as a commanding general, violating the very rudiments of strategy, to wit, (*that an officer, when attacked, has to defend himself under all circumstances, and at all hazards,* while he *who makes an attack, before he is completely and in every particular fully prepared,* acts the part of a fool); we think we are justified in the expectation that, taking so enormous responsibilities upon himself, in making a forward movement with so badly prepared an army, the general will exercise the utmost care in giving all the necessary orders and instructions, in so precise and perfect a manner that, at least, many of the organic deficiencies of his army may thereby be neutralized. We deeply regret that justice to the various officers who held command under General McDowall, and to their brave soldiers, compel us to say, that the unmilitary orders issued by him, have as much if not more to do with the disastrous result of the affair of Bull Run, than the want of proper organization, drill and preparation of the army before it left Washington. A commanding General when about to go into a battle of his own selection, at his own time and on his own battle field, has nothing to do with his troops on the march towards the battle field; he needs the troops on the battle field, where he assumes command in person over the entire army, while up to that moment the command and the responsibilities are with the commanders of the various corps. The order of a Commanding General, directing the various corps of his army to move to a certain position, by him designated to each of them respectively, in or near the battle field, ought therefore distinctly to state the time when each corps shall *reach its respective position*. This time alone *can and ought to be fixed by the Comanding General*. It has to be left to the better judgement of the commanders of the various corps, to their intimate knowledge of the character and physique of their troops, of the distance to be marched, of the condition of the roads, and so forth; to determine when they *have to commence* the march for their position on the field, to reach it at the time fixed by the Commanding General. This rule General McDowell has violated in his order to the Commanders of Divisions, in which, instead of fixing the time when the various divisions were respectively to *reach* the positions by him designated to them, he says: *the divisions were ordered to march at half-past two o'clock, A. M., so as to arrive on the ground early in the day and thus avoid the heat*. This order leaves the the time when he wants the troops in their position completely undecided, and takes the responsibilities, the blame for delay in stopping to drink, and all the disorganizing consequences, to which he in his report refers, from the shoulders of the Division Commanders and puts it upon those of General McDowell, who had no right to say in his report that "*the divisions were between two and three hours behind the time appointed.*" He had, according to his own statements, *not appointed any time* at all when *they were to be in position*. These two to three hours behind time, tell fearfully against the General. The unmilitary order for all the divisions to commence the march at the same time, of necessity caused collision and confusion among the various divisions at the outset; exposed the troops on the march to the very heat which was to be avoided, and consequently delayed the commencement, and the termination of the engagement, about three hours beyond the time, when, under a competent General it would have taken place; if he ever had placed himself, under the existing circumstances, in the undesirable position of fighting a battle. These three hours are the very identical few hours, which in General McDowell's own opinion, and according to his statement, in the finishing sentence of his report, *would have secured success to the Union army*, and consequently would have prevented its destruction It may not be superfluous here to note the fact, that according to General McDowell's report, the frequently talked of rebel fortifications at and near Manassas, had never been reached by any portion of the Union army, and therefore remained as much *terra incognita* after the 21st day of July, 1861, as they had been up to that date.

When the alarm, confusion and consternation caused by the affair at Bull Run had to some extent subsided, and when General McClellan commenced the organization of a new army, General McDowell was put in command of a division of the army on the Potomac, whence he was promoted to the command of a corps d'armee and a Major-General.

Next to the Department of the Rappahannock, and partly belonging thereto, we come to the District of Columbia, over which Brigadier-General James S. Wadsworth was appointed military Governor. The protection, and, in case of emergency, the defence of the City of Washington, with all the important government records and treasure, had been perfected by the construction of some thirty earth works, of more or less strength, mounting in the aggregate a very imposing number of guns, of the heaviest calibre and most improved pattern, and garrisoned by quite a respectable army, composed of infantry, cavalry and mostly of artillery. The circumstance that the regular population of the District was not only considerably increased by the war, that the floating population consists, to a very great extent, in commands and detachments from almost all the regiments that compose the army of the United States, that all these troops, during their sojourn in Washington, are to a greater or smaller extent, placed under the control of the military Governor, makes the office of the last named functionary one of great importance. It can be properly held only by a person of military experience, great tact, sense of justice, and superior executive talent.

Brigadier-General Wadsworth had joined the army under the President's first call for volunteers, with one of the militia regiments of the State of New York; he was promoted a Major, and, as General McDowell says in his report of Bull Run, did that General the honor to be one of his personal staff. When the despair and consternation caused by the Bull Run affair gradually began to give way to a feeling of greater security, and more cheerful expectations, produced by the vigorous manner in which the reorganization of the totally demoralised army by General McClellan was carried on, those persons more or less engaged in Bull Run gradually became visible again in the public places in and around Washington; many of them considering it unpardonable in General McClellan to insist upon it that the army should be completely organised, armed, equipped, officered and drilled, as well as provided with all the necessary auxilliaries; that *en fine* it should be as different from the so-called army that left Washington to go to Bull's Run as black is from white, before he would lead it against an enemy, (who in addition to the self-reliance and confidence gained by his success at Bull's Run, had erected and manned at and around Manassas Junction numerous fortifications which at the time of the Bull Run disaster were already so formidable that not one man of McDowell's army approached them, and which since that fatal day had been continually extended and strengthened). Among those disapproving of General McClellan's strategy General Wadsworth was prominent, and he is said to have publicly declared that McClellan's army was strong enough at any time to march against and over the rebel fortifications at Manassas whenever that General would say the word forward, and that because McClellan did not go and attack these fortifications he had become his declared enemy.

What opportunities General Wadsworth has had, to form a correct opinion of the strength required by an army to take and march over the Manassas fortifications we do not know. It is well known that neither the latter gentleman nor any other officer of our army had ever seen these fortifications, neither before, at, nor since Bull Run had afforded to General Wadsworth only an opportunity to see the mismanagement, weakness, repulse and panic of an army, but not its strength or its application and success. He had never seen any other army make a successful advance against fortifications of any kind It is the opinion universally expressed in Washington that, (without considering for a moment whether he was a tall a competent judge in military affairs, without recollecting that to speak disrespectfully and with contempt of a superior officer is under the articles of war a serious offence, deserving punishment, and that, as general-in-chief of the army, General McClellan was the superior of Brigadier-General Wadsworth) the latter was among the loudest who accused General McClellan of inactivity, of want of talent, of dash and of military qualification in general, and who used all his influence for the purpose of opposing and crippling the execution of his plans for the campaign of 1862. However self-confident he may have been as to his superior judgment in military affairs regarding *offensive* movements, it seems that the confidence of the President and Secretary of War in his talents and qualification to direct the *defense* of a place surrounded by fortifications, even at that early part of the campaign, was by no means equal to his own, because his military department was embodied in the Department of the Rappahannock at the very first formation thereof, and the military command vested in General McDowell. The left wing of the army was occupied by the army of the Potomac, leaning with the left on the bank of that river. Major-General George B. McClellan had command of this army, which he himself had organised and in every respect prepared and militarised from its first formation.

It has been so frequently and in so many places, and by so many persons of all political parties, publicly stated—it has never been contradicted, and it therefore can not be doubted—that according to McClellan's plan for the campaign of 1862, the army of the Potomac as well, as the grand army in the West under General Halleck, were not to commence their simultaneous general movements against the rebel forces before the month of April, because it was impossible for the armies to be in every respect completely prepared for the great work laid out for them. That the President, who was completely familiar with McClellan's plan, had fully approved of and sanctioned it; had in the early spring of the year, lost the strength of will to rely upon his own better judgment, and yielding to the opinions of others, had pressed McClellan to deviate from his well-considered plans. The latter (convinced of the disastrous consequences which a yielding against his own well matured conviction would carry with it, and remembering the advice given him by his veteran predecessor, Winfield Scott, in their parting interview at the railroad depot at Washington, "*never to allow himself to be influenced by the opinion of others, against his own deliberate judgment,*" had resisted all the force brought to bear on him, and had refused to order a premature forward movement. That in consequence thereof, McClellan was deprived of the command-in-chief of the army, left in command of the army of the Potomac only; and the new independent Departments were created. McClellan, after having explained and demonstrated all the necessary evil consequences of a forward movement, before the time fixed upon by him; a good soldier as he is, had, when he ceased to be General-in-chief, punctually executed the orders received from the Commander-in-Chief, advanced with the army of the Potomac from Arlington Heights towards Centreville, Manassas and Warrenton, and directed McDowell's corps towards Fredericksburg. He then, with his entire army, except McDowell's corps of four divisions, returned to Alexandria and embarked thence for Fortress Monroe and the Peninsula. From April until August, 1862, his army was entirely isolated from the armies of the other Departments in Virginia.

For the complete military history and review of the operations of the army of the Potomac on the Peninsula, we refer our readers to a pamphlet published by H. Dexter, 113 Nassau street, New-York, entitled "Major General George B. McClellan, from August 1861 to August 1862," which gives a lucid history of the services General McClellan has rendered to the country.

Having examined the positions of the different corps of the army in Virginia, designated to them by the President's War Orders, having despatched the army of the Potomac under McClellan to the Peninsula, and having become acquainted with the commanding generals of the various corps, we will now try to find out what military results were to be obtained by the various corps, and how far the commanding generals succeeded in achieving what they were expected to perform.

The main object of the campaign of 1862 in Virginia was to get possession of Richmond; the part, in the execution of this plan, assigned to Generals McDowell, Banks and Fremont, was to gain possession of the Rappahannock river from the Potomac to Fredericksburg; to drive the small rebel force under General Jackson still in the Shenandoah valley, across the Shanandoah, then take possession of Gordonville thereby (destroying the line of communication between Richmond and the Virginia Central Railroad), to secure the double facilities of the Orange and Alexandria and the Richmond and Fredericksburg Railroads for our army supplies of every description, in the advance of a corps of our forces by way of Hanover Court House, to Richmond.

In the execution of this plan General McDowell's corps had been left near Warrenton Junction, whence he moved toward Fredericksburg, while at the same time a few gunboats of the Potomac flotilla passed up the Rappahannock and destroyed a rebel battery near Lowry's Point. A few days later, General McDowell's corps, without meeting any rebel force strong enough to offer resistance to his advance, reached Falmouth, opposite Fredericksburg, on the 18th of April, after the small rebel force had succeeded in destroying the bridge across the river—not, however, with the intention of disputing the passage of the river, but merely to retard the forward movement of the union army, which they of course expected to be intended, because the municipal authorities of Fredericksburg were not prevented from offering to surrender the city upon a guarantee of protection to private property, which condition was granted by General Huger, the commander of the forces that first reached the place.

General Banks, as soon as he had been vested with the command of the Department of the Shanandoah, went to work to clear it from the enemy. He advanced his troops to the vicinity of Winchester, where, on the 22d day of March, General Shields' division brought on an engagement with the forces under General Jackson, in which General Shields was wounded and put *hors du combat*, by almost the first shell fired against our troops. General Banks, who had been on his way to Washington where he had been summoned, reached the battle-field in time to resume command, and in an engagement of two days, in which the troops of General Jackson were to great advantage placed behind stone fences, whence our army had to drive them at the point of the bayonet, he compelled the rebels to retreat with a considerable loss in killed, wounded and artillery, pursued by the Union army. The position of his troops, under protection of the stone fences, won General Jackson the surname Stonewall, by which, since that time, he has been generally designated. The battle at Winchester was soon followed by one at Strasburg, where Jackson had made a stand; but he had to retreat from here, driven as at Winchester, at the point of the bayonet. He made another stand at Woodstock, but had again to retreat before the cold steel of the Union army. Although he had been considerably reinforced, and although he destroyed all the bridges behind him, and thereby considerably increased the difficulties General Banks had to encounter in his pursuit, nevertheless he had to retreat from Mt. Jackson, from New-Market, and finally from Harrisonburg, after having made a stand, and having been forced in a general engagement of all his forces, to yield every one of these positions to the army under General Banks. From Harrisonburg he retreated toward Staunton, crossed the Shenandoah and destroyed the bridge; thus he prevented General Banks from pursuing him immediately, and he even kept him for a while in ignorance of the direction in which he had withdrawn, leaving the impression on his mind that the rebel army had moved towards Gordonsville. The several battles and engagements above mentioned, and the march from Winchester to Harrisonburg had occupied a period of about six weeks; and after General Banks' corps had driven Jackson from Harrisonburg, and after the latter had crossed the river and destroyed the bridge behind him, there commenced a period of inactivity in General Banks' army which surprised his numerous friends and admirers at the time, but which was explained by subsequent events.

The troops forming the command of Major General John C. Fremont, of the mountain Department, had to be concentrated from various parts of the country. The staff of the Commanding General had to be organized, and the machinery for the management, subsistance and transportation of a *corps d'armee* had to be put in proper working order before the corps could be in condition to take the field with any prospect of success. All these causes operated to the result that while General Banks' corps was gaining victory after victory, the country did not hear of any movements in the mountain department.

General McDowell, after having occupied Fredericksburg, where he found a considerable amount of grain and forage stored by the enemy, had the bridges across the river rebuilt, and put his pickets just beyond the city, so as to be secure against a surprise. At the same time we find him a frequent passenger on the railroad, travelling from Fredericksburg to Washington and back again. Thus time passed on, till General Stonewall Jackson, in retreating before Gen. Banks, crosses the Shenandoah, and leaves that General in doubt as to his exact position. General Banks, who was always with his army and in the saddle, reported to the Secretary of War that Jackson was very near his front, contemplating an attack. General McDowell, who had to divide his time between Fredericksburg and Washington, reported at the same time that he had heard that Jackson was in his front, and he asked for reinforcements, to feel perfectly secure in his position, although he had already a by far larger force than Gen. Banks, although he had not lost anything in battles which he had not fought, while Banks' corps was considerably reduced by losses in the various battles above mentioned. The Secretary of War, was by these contradictory reports, placed in a position actually to direct the movements of armies before the enemy, to become responsible for the success or defeat of the cause of the Union, on the field in question, and for the lives of thousands of brave men. They joined the army in the reasonable expectation of being put under command of experienced military men, but not to be sacrificed by the assumption of the control of armies by a completely unqualified person, a position really embarrassing to a man without military knowledge or experience. It can not surprise anybody that Mr. Stanton's order was exactly the reverse from what it ought to have been. He ordered Gen. Banks, 1st, to send 15,000 men, under Gen. Shields, to reinforce Gen. McDowell, at Fredericksburg; and 2d, with the rest of his troops, 4000 infantry, 1500 cavalry, ten Parrot guns and six smooth bores, to fall back upon Strasburg. In compliance with this order, Gen. Shields had passed safely through Manassas Gap, and joined McDowell; but Col. Kearney, with a Maryland regiment, following over the same route, was intercepted near Front Royal, about ten miles east of Strasburg, by Jackson's troops, who had followed in pursuit, the moment he saw the retrograde movement of Gen. Banks, and were badly cut to pieces. Jackson then attacked with his 15,000 men, Gen. Banks, near Strasburg, on the 24th of May, early in the morning, and forced him, in a continuous retreat, over the same route over which he himself had been driven about four weeks ago; and then still further on across the Potomac, which Banks crossed in perfect order, and reached Williamsport, Maryland, May 26th, in the evening. Jackson took about fifty wagons, large quantities of stores, ammunition and uniforms, stored at Winchester; but, thanks to the superior discipline in Banks' corps, thanks to the full confidence of the officers and men in their General, and thanks to the superior combination and good generalship of the commander of the Department of the Shenandoah, Stonewall Jackson did not succeed in taking his entire army prisoners, nor in driving them into the Potomac, and thus destroying them. One or the other he would, in all probability, have accomplished, against a commander not so properly qualified as N. P. Banks. Gen. McDowell, in the meanwhile, remained undisturbed at Fredericksburg, and saw not the ghost of an enemy. This raid of Stonewall Jackson perplexed the Secretary of War completely; he telegraphed to Governor Andrew, of Massachusetts, "the army of Banks is completely routed, and the Capital in danger." Such statements, coming from such a personage, although they were not founded in truth, caused a panic in Wall street, cost the country millions and millions, and spread consternation all over the land. Immediately after this alarming intelligence had produced its effect, the country was given to understand that Banks' retreat had been a mere matter of strategy, that Jackson was bagged in the Shenandoah Valley, and would never get out of it alive. Generals Fremont and McDowell were ordered to move at once and to intercept Jackson's retreat from the valley at all hazards. Both these Generals moved; Gen. Fremont had the misfortune to lead his army wrong, to lose his way, and to arrive at Strasburg on the 2d of June, just in time to be too late to intercept Jackson, who had constructed a rope barricade, across which a large number of Fremont's cavalry stumbled, and were wounded and taken prisoners. Next evening, Fremont came up with the rear guard of Jackson's army, and in connection with Gen. Shields' troops, who had arrived from Fredericksburg, and over whom he assumed command had several engagements with the rebels, under command of Ashby, in which the latter had all the advantage, and finally eluded Fremont so completely, that for several days neither Fremont nor Shields, nor McDowell, nor the Secretary of War, had the faintest idea of his whereabouts. All these Generals kept their troops resting on their arms, believing the enemy to be just in front of them. Jackson, meantime, was far away on his way to Hanover Court House, where, after resting and recruiting his army, he made, on the 26th day of June, the attack on the right wing of the Army of the Potomac.

Thus, of all the work laid out to be performed by the commanders of the Departments of the Rappahannock, Shenandoah, and the Mountain Department, nothing whatever had been accomplished; McDowell was still in Fredericksburg, which he had never left, except to go back to Washington. Fremont had accomplished nothing; and Banks, although he had distinguished himself as a commanding general, in the offensive as well as in the retreat, had, by the interference of incompetent superiors, been compelled to abandon the advantages already gained. Mr. Stanton, relying, according to his doctrine in the *Tribune* letter, upon the Spirit of the Lord, upon inspiration, upon the blessing of Providence, and upon Joshua, to organize victories and plan the battles for him, had, of course, utterly failed in the task voluntarily undertaken to control armies in the field by receiving frequent reports from and giving orders to the commanders of independent corps. The necessary co-operation of all or any of the above corps in the advance upon Richmond by the army of the Potomac, which had been solemnly promised, had not even been attempted; the success of that army had thereby been endangered, and the country had suffered enormous in men and means.

In this emergency, the President considered it important to re-establish the unity of command over the corps of McDowell, Banks, and Fremont, which had been destroyed by his War Order No. 3. For that purpose he consolidated them into the army of Virginia, and appointed Major-General John Pope commanding general thereof, June 25th. Fremont to command the first, Banks the second, and McDowell the third army corps of the army of Virginia.

Immediately after the announcement of this appointment, General John C. Fremont sent in the resignation of his command, because he considered his dignity offended by the appointment, as commanding general over him, of an officer whom he out-ranked. His resignation was accepted, and after the command of the first corps of the army had been tendered to and had been declined by General Rufus King, Major-General Franz Sigel was appointed to that command.

It may not be out of place here to mention that the authority *to appoint a general of lower rank to command over officers out-ranking him*—an authority interfering materially with the universally established military rules, calculated, when exercised, in nine cases out of ten, to cause mischief and ill will, to destroy harmony and cordial co-operation, and thereby to undermine elements essential for the success of any army—that this authority was given to the President by an act of Congress, originating with, and carried principally by the votes of, the friends of General Fremont, with the intention, it was said, to see General McClellan—who would not allow anybody to interfere with his official business—superseded by General Fremont, whom he out-ranked. As if Nemesis had willed it, the first instance in which the President thought himself justified to exercise this dangerous authority, he had to exercise it against General Fremont. How far the step taken by the latter was taken with good grace towards his friends, is a question on which opinions may differ. That General Fremont, as a soldier, in the face of the enemy, at a moment when his country's cause was in danger, when every man was asked and expected to do his whole duty, by act, by encouragement in word and example, acted wrong, unpatriotic, and set a bad example to every officer in the army, even if his resignation had been justifiable by strict interpretation of established military rule—on that point we say there can be but one opinion. Of all the Generals in the army, John C. Fremont was the only one *who had no right to complain of or take umbrage at the exercise of the President's authority to supersede him by a junior officer*, because General Fremont had been deprived of his command on grave charges in October, 1861. The act vesting the President with the above mentioned unexampled authority *had been passed soon after, and was the law of the land.* When, at the urgent solicitations of his friends, the President tendered him the command of the Mountain Department, the General was fully aware of the existence of the act in question, and it was his duty, as a soldier and as a man, at that time, to consider and to decide whether or not, with such an authority in the President's hands, he thought it proper to accept a command in the army? In accepting it, he knowingly and willingly submitted to take his chances of being hurt by the exercise of the President's authority, and waived all his right to complain in case he should be hurt.

Military law considers resignation before the enemy an act of cowardice, and makes no distinction between officers of higher or lower rank. General Pope says on the subject, from Headquarters, Army of Virginia, Warrenton, July 30, 1862: " No resignation of any officer whatever will be accepted, except upon medical certificate of the most conclusive character, or proof of worthlessness ; it is therefore to be distinctly understood, that any officer of this army whose resignation has been accepted without medical certificate, has proved himself worthless and incompetent."

When, in consequence of the utter failure of the summer campaign, President Lincoln had called for 300,000 volunteers, when a mass meetng was held in the city of New York, for the purpose of encouraging a hearty response to the President's call, on the 15th of July, 1862, a fortnight after he had resigned his command before the enemy, had set a bad example to every officer, soldier, and patriot, and all that, as we have shown, without any just cause; when he ought to have hidden himself till time had made his act pass from the memory of the people, on that day John C. Fremont, in the uniform of a Major-General, appeared on stand No. 5, Union Square, and made a speech, asking the people to enlist as volunteers, and to sacrifice their lives on the altar of their conntry—who can wonder that the Government had to resort to a draft?

General John Pope, as a captain in the regular army, was appointed by the War Department one of the officers to escort President Lincoln to Washington. When the rebellion broke out, he was made a brigadier-general, and had a command in Missouri. When General Halleck took command of the department of the Mississippi, he sent Pope with a corps of about 12,000 men, to operate in the rear of New Madrid, while the gunboats made an attack in front ; this accomplished, without any resistance by the rebels, General Pope moved farther to the Arkansas line, to assist in the reduction of Island No. 10, in the Mississippi. General Schuyler Hamilton, who had command under him, suggested, as the General states in his report, to cut a canal through the swamp and bayou, for the purpose of sending transports and a gunboat below the island. Colonel Ripley, commanding an engineer regiment, had the canal dug by his men, and General Pope's corps was enabled to embark and cross the river. Some gunboats from above had ran the gauntlet of the enemy's batteries, and could protect the crossing army, against the attack of any rebel craft, sent up from Memphis to the support of Island No. 10. This crossing of the Mississippi, without the loss of a single man either in embarkation or disembarkation of the troops, although not interfered with by any hostile demonstration, was, nevertheless, a great success. But even this was eclipsed by a still more wonderful performance, next succeeding the disembarkation of Pope's corps on the left bank of the river, to wit, by the capture of some 6,000 rebels on their retreat from the evacuation of Island No. 10, without firing a shot. When General Halleck concentrated his army for the purpose of besieging Corinth, General Pope's command became part of the besieging force, and entered Corinth with the rest, after Beauregard's army had evacuated the place. This accomplished, active operation of the grand army of the West came to a stand-still. Almost all the generals holding command therein (with the exception of Generals Buell and Grant, who always remained with their troops), proceeded to the city of Washington, for purposes best known to themselves. Thus General Pope happened to be in Washington when the President needed somebody to bring unity in the operations of the three army corps above mentioned. He was promoted a major-general, and appointed to the command of the newly-created army of Virginia.

The achievements of General Pope out West appearing to great advantage—for distance lends enchantment to the view—but by no means indicating any qualification for a command of an army against an enemy, had, nevertheless, the effect, that his appointment to the command of the army of Virginia, was generally considered as a proper one.

On the fourteenth day of July, General Pope issued the following order to the officers and soldiers of the army of Virginia:

WASHINGTON, *July* 14, 1862.

TO THE OFFICERS AND SOLDIERS OF THE ARMY OF VIRGINIA:

By special assignment of the President of the United States, I have assumed the command of this army.

I have spent two weeks in learning your whereabouts, your condition, and your wants; in preparing you for active operations, and in placing you in positions from which you can act promptly and to the purpose.

I have come to you from the West, where we have always seen the backs of our enemies, from an army whose business it has been to seek the adversary, and to beat him when found, whose policy has been attack, and not defense.

In but one instance has the enemy been able to place our Western armies in a defensive attitude.

I presume that I have been called here to pursue the same system, and to lead you against the enemy.

It is my purpose to do so, and that speedily.

I am sure you long for an opportunity to win the distinction you are capable of achieving. That opportunity I shall endeavor to give you.

Meantime, I desire you to dismiss from your minds certain phrases which I am sorry to find so much in vogue among you.

I hear constantly of taking strong positions and holding them—of lines of retreat and bases of supplies. Let us discard such ideas.

The strongest position a soldier should desire to occupy, is one from which he can most easily advance against the enemy.

Let us study the probable lines of retreat of our opponents, and leave our own to take care of themselves.

Let us look before, and not behind.

Success and glory are in the advance.

Disaster and shame lurk in the rear,

Let us act on this understanding, and it is safe to predict that your banners shall be inscribed with many a glorious deed, and that your names will be dear to your countrymen forever.

JOHN POPE,
Major-General Commanding.

This order fell like a thunder-clap upon the mind of all reflecting persons, but in particular upon military men.

Proper conduct under all, even the most difficult and perplexing circumstances, is one of the fundamental and indispensible requirements for an officer, of whatever rank, but in particular for an officer commanding a corps or an army, so much so that *conduct unbecoming an officer* is one of the gravest charges to be brought against him. To what extent proper conduct of an officer is required, may be best illustrated by the proceedings of a Court-Martial, held in New York in reference to charges preferred against the officer commanding the United States forces, embarked in New York, on board the steamer San Francisco, shipwrecked, and rescued by the captain of the British ship Three Bells.

An officer who lacks proper conduct, in the most ordinary affairs of life, is not qualified for, and is unreliable in, any command, but in particular is he utterly disqualified for command of an army. General Pope's order of June 14, 1862, is improper from beginning to end. The second sentence is, to say the least, discourteous to Generals McDowell, Banks, and Fremont, because it insinuates that these generals, although in the field for some months, had left their armies *unprepared for active operations*, and had kept them in positions from which they could not *act promptly or to the purpose*. Sentences three, four, five, six, seven and eight, contain nothing but self-conceit and bravado. Our armies in the West would not deserve the credit for gallantry, for which they are justly distinguished, if they *had always seen the backs of the enemy*—that is, if the enemy had always run away. It is a peculiar fact that at New Madrid, and at Island No. 10, General Pope had to operate in the rear of the enemy, and therefore only saw their backs, while others saw the enemy's face. At Corinth he saw Beauregard's back, but at a great distance, inasmuch as the latter had marched nine miles with his main army before Halleck occupied the place. Sentences nine, ten, eleven, twelve, thirteen, fourteen and fifteen, in imitation of Mr. Stanton's *Tribune* letter, contain a slur on General McClellan, General Pope's superior in rank; an officer who, at the time when the latter, in his order, forgot his duty to a brother officer, had led his army to beard the lion in his own den, had taken Yorktown, had won the battles of Williamsburg and Fair Oaks, and had never met with a single defeat. These sentences express opinions in open contradiction to the very fundamental principles of strategy in general, and to the revised army regulations of 1861, in particular. Principles, the violation of which caused the disasters at Belmont to Generals Grant and McClernand; while, by the strict adherence to them, Beauregard saved his army at Bowling Green, at Columbus, at Island No. 10, and at Corinth, although at every one of these places, our generals predicted his capture. Principles which no soldier has ever violated without being severely punished for it. That a commander, proclaiming the principles contained in this order, could never fulfil the predictions contained in its closing sentences, is not to be wondered at.

Ten days after the above mentioned order had astonished the country, General Pope issued, on the 26th of July, the following:

HEAD-QUARTERS ARMY OF VIRGINIA,
WASHINGTON, *July* 26, 1862.

Captain Samuel L. Harrison, of the Ninety-Fifth Regiment of New York volunteers, is reported by his commanding general as having deserted his company on the 21st of this month, and gone to New York. A reward of five cents is offered for his apprehension.

By order of   MAJOR-GENERAL POPE.
GEORGE D. RUGGLES, Chief of Staff.

This order is unmilitary, and a palpable violation of the revised army regulations of 1861, which, in sections 20, 24, and 50, direct a commander how to catch, how to try, and how to punish a deserter. They are just as binding to the general commanding, as they are to the youngest drummer-boy in the army. It is a premeditated insult offered by General Pope to all officers of the army, as a class,—an insult, that in any other army would cause the general either to be court-martialed and cashiered, or to be shot at by every officer as long as there was anything left of him (Gen. Pope). Some six years ago, for an expression, by far less insulting than the order in question, *Lieutenant-General* Von Plehwe was shot dead by *Second* lieutenant Von Jachman, in a duel fought under the sanction of the *Council of Honor*, every member of the council being present at the duel. The *Court of Honor* who tried the case, honorably acquitted the principal, the seconds, and every member of the *Council of Honor*, from a violation of the laws against duelling; and the King of Prussia, to whose army both the combatants belonged, although he referred the verdict of the first *Court of Honor* successively to two different courts, did not succeed in having the same materially amended. Not until every officer in our army, high or low in rank, recognizes in every other officer a brother in arms, whom he treats as such, and whose honor is as sacred to him as his own (till by his conduct he forfeits this recognition and thereby his commission), not until then can we expect our army to be raised to its fullest discipline and military efficiency.

The President, for reasons best known to himself, on the 11th day of August, immediately on his return from a visit to the army of the Potomac at Harrison's Landing, appointed Major General Halleck General-in-Chief of the Army of the United States, and his arrival in Washington was daily expected. General Pope, nevertheless, thought proper, without awaiting this arrival, which took place July 22d, to issue, July 18th, the following Orders No. 5 and 6:

General Order—No. 5.

HEADQUARTERS, ARMY OF VIRGINIA, }
Washington, July 18, 1862. }

Hereafter, as far as practicable, the troops of this command will subsist upon the country in which their operations are carried on. In all cases supplies for this purpose will be taken by the officers to whose department they properly belong, under the orders of the commanding officers of the troops for whose use they are intended. Vouchers will be given to the owners, stating on their face that they will be payable at the conclusion of the war, upon sufficient testimony being furnished that such owners have been loyal citizens of the United States since the date of the vouchers. Whenever it is known that supplies can be furnished in any district of the country where the troops are to operate, the use of trains for carrying subsistence will be dispensed with as far as possible.

By command of Major General POPE.
GEORGE D. RUGGLES, Colonel, A. A. G. and Chief of Staff.

General Order—No. 6.

HEADQUARTERS, DEPARTMENT OF VIRGINIA,
Washington, July 18, 1862.

Hereafter, in any operations of the cavalry forces in this command, no supply or baggage trains of any description will be used, unless so stated specially in the order for the movement. Two days' cooked rations will be carried on the persons of the men, and all villages or neighborhoods through which they pass will be laid under contribution in the manner specified by general order No. 5, current series for these headquarters, for the subsistence of men and horses. Movements of cavalry must always be made with celerity, and no delay in such movements will be excused hereafter on any pretext.

Whenever the order for the movement of any portion of this army emanates from these headquarters, the time of marching, and that to be consumed in the execution of the duty, will be expressly designated, and no departure therefrom will be permitted to pass unnoticed, without the gravest and most conclusive reasons. Commanding officers will be held responsible for strict and prompt compliance with every provision of this order.

By command of   Major General POPE.
GEO. D. RUGGLES, Colonel, A. A. G. and Chief of Staff.

The rebel government retaliated by declaring that whenever General Pope or any of his officers should be taken prisoners, they should not be treated as prisoners of war, but should be put in close confinement and be hanged. In his army this order caused so much lawless conduct that General Pope found himself under the necessity to issue another order, August 14th, amending the previous one, in conformity with an order on the same subject, issued August 9th, by General McClellan. All these orders having been launched, General Pope finally left the city of Washington to join his army in the field, July 26th, 1862. Before this change of quarters he had ordered a movement by a part of his army under General Hatch, which resulted in a *report* all over the country, that he had taken possession of the town of Gordonsville, Va., a point of the highest strategical importance to the rebels. When the truth of the matter became known, Gordonsville had not been seen; on the contrary, for want of proper instructions, an important bridge on the road thereto had been destroyed by our own men, and thereby had been converted into protection for the rebels against an attack from us, and into an obstacle to our progress in the proper direction.

The idea of gaining possession of Gordonsville (which at the time the first movement of Pope's army took place was occupied only by an insignificant rebel force, and might easily have been taken by a bold dash) seems to us, to be one of the principal causes of the disastrous results of the short campaign between the Rappahannock and the Potomac. Having failed to accomplish in July what at that time ought to have been done, General Pope did not take into proper consideration that the moment the movement of General Hatch was reported to Richmond, a force sufficient to hold Gordonsville was despatched to protect it, and to defeat all and any of Pope's operations in that direction. The commander of the rebel forces, entrusted with the execution of this order, was too good a soldier to remain idle at Gordonsville, when, on his arrival there, he found the Union army still spread over a vast territory, and far on the opposite side of the Rapidan. He intended to keep Pope as far away from his "pasture grounds" as possible. He therefore occupied and strongly posted himself at and near Cedar Mountain, keeping Robin's creek in front, and surrounding on three sides a narrow plateau intersected by "Cedar Spring creek," and by two roads leading to Culpepper Court House and Sperryville. Into this plateau, which formed an elongated circle segment, the base towards the Union army and about a mile in length, General Pope, on the 9th day of August, sent the corps of General Banks, which, as we have seen, he had drawn from the Shanandoah valley, with instructions to hold this position while he himself, with General McDowell, remained at Culpepper, some seven miles distant, ordering Sigel with his corps from Sperryville also to move to Culpepper. Banks had hardly taken position when the rebels opened upon him from both flanks and in front, with heavy artillery, placed in masked positions on a high elevation, which at the same time commanded the *only two bridges over Cedar creek, in his rear*, over which he could retreat, or over which succor could reach him (see map of battle field). The General saw at once that to stand on the defensive would be destruction by the enemy's cross-fire; to retreat would only hasten this destruction, in the attempt to pass the two bridges above mentioned. A brave, intelligent soldier, and a skillful commander, he at once adopted the only plan which gave a chance of success, that is, to dislodge the enemy from his strong position by attacking it. With fearful loss he gradually succeeded, by the brilliant gallantry of his troops, to force the enemy into a retrogade movement. In the evening General Pope appeared at the battle field, followed by Sigel's and part of McDowell's corps, to within about two miles of the battle field, and for the first time discovered that the battle field was so narrow, and the roads leading to it so few, that it was impossible to move fresh troops forward and withdraw Banks' corps; Gen. Banks had to fight it out to the bitter end with his ex hausted troops, although some 20,000 men stood within a short distance of him eager, but unable to march to his assistance, because Pope had sent him in to a bag. Night terminated the slaughter; the rebels withdrew a short distance to a near mountain ridge; Banks occupied the position in which he had first been attacked, and apparently both parties attended to their dead and wounded. We say apparently, because the rebels saw at once that with the concentration of the corps of Banks, Sigel and McDowell, at and near Cedar Mountain, Gen. Pope had left open to them their old highway in the Shenandoah Valley. They, therefore, left a comparatively small force, it is said, under command of Ewell, on the Rapidan, and between Sperryville and Culpepper, to entertain Pope's army, to advance or to retreat as occasion may require, but under all circumstances to keep him there as long as possible, and to hang on his heels in case he should retreat. Gen. Burnside, who had joined McClellan's army after the seven days' battle, had landed at Acquia Creek, and joined Pope. McClellan, with the entire Army of the Potomac, had left Harrison's Landing almost on the same day on which Banks distinguished himself at Cedar Mountain, by saving a part of his army, in a position selected by Pope, where, in nine cases out of ten, his entire corps would be destroyed. The rebel leaders were thereby relieved of all anxiety about the safety of their own capital. This movement, from a military point of view, by whomsoever it may have been ordered, must be considered one of the greatest strategical blunders during the entire campaign. For a large army, the only military line of approach to Richmond, is the line of the James River; the line by Fredericksburg we consider a military impossibility, on account of the constant destruction by the rebels of the line of communication, and on account of the impossibility to support a large army at so great a distance from a *water base*.

Napoleon, when, contrary to his well matured plan to go into winter quarters at Wilna, he advanced into the interior of the enemy's country, towards Moscow, overlooked this very difficulty. The impossibility to protect, in the enemy's country, a line of communication a hundred miles or more in length, and in consequence thereof the almost incessant attacks of the French army by Cossacks, who swarmed around them like bees; destroyed every bridge, thereby retarding his march beyond all calculation, made his retreat one of unparallelled disaster, almost annihilation, compared with which, the effect of the climate alone upon the army, in unobstructed rapid marches, would have been insignificant. The rebel cavalry, under General Stuart, we fear, would be the Cossacks to any army that will march from Washington via Fredericksburg, to Richmond.

This impossibility alone, justifies Gen. Halleck in not following Beauregard when he retreated from Corinth. Halleck's army was then the largest Union army ever concentrated in the field; it had had no battle since Pittsburg Landing, was in fine condition, was well supplied with everything necessary, had experience and success on his side; while the rebel army had nothing to show but want, retreats and reverses. The impossibility of supporting so large an army as his in the enemy's exhausted country, away from a water base, forced the General to allow Beauregard to move wherever he saw fit to go, to rest, to recruit, and to reinforce Richmond in time for the battles against the Army of the Potomac, which army would have been destroyed, had not General McClellan, by his genius, by his energetic movements, his gallantry, dash, and military excellence, triumphed over the combined talent and bravery of the rebel leaders and their armies. The same reasons that prevented General Halleck from following Beauregard's army on their way from Corinth to Richmond, prevent the movement of a large army from Washington, by way of Fredericksburg, for the occupation of Richmond. Relieved on the James River of the army of the Potomac, (which reached Alexandria soon after the middle of August, and was, in its single corps and divisions, separately assigned to the army of Virginia under General Pope, so that McClellan had hardly a corporal's guard left him,) the rebels sent a large army under General Lee, by way of Gordonsville and Staunton, in the Shenandoah Valley, thence to Manassas Gap, and through Thoroughfare Gap by way of Bull Run and Centerville to Washington. This road to the national Capitol, upon which the rebel army had been moving, more than once during the war, had been left completely unprotected by General Pope. He had marched according to his ideas of *concentration*, placed his entire army in a small corner of his department, and carried his horrors of looking to the rear, so far as not even to dare to look to his flanks. He had, without the least idea of a reserve corps, or of the safety of Washington, pending battles in close proximity, drawn the entire force under Burnside, and almost the entire army of the Potomac, into the same narrow compass of his strategy, in which they had several engagements, all of them terminating unfavorably for the Union army, the reports of his brilliant victories to the contrary notwithstanding. At the eleventh hour, (after

General Lee had, by a cavalry expedition under General Stuart, which captured Pope's tent and all its contents, convinced himself, that his road was perfectly clear from Pope's soldiers;) a fortunate accident placed General Pope in possession of a letter from General Lee, containing his orders for the movement on Washington, above mentioned. He now tried to dispute the passage of Thoroughfare Gap, by sending a corps to that place, but it is too late; the rebels force the passage, and Pope actually finds a portion of Lee's army between himself and Washington; fortunately, the rebel corps was too small to resist the combined forces under Pope, and he succeeded in placing his army again between Washington and the enemy, but only to be attacked and driven from position to position, during five days almost uninterrupted fighting. Gainsville, Manassas Junction, the old battle field of Bull Run, Centerville, and Fairfax Court House, are in quick succession the scenes, not of well devised battles, but of a rough and tumble fight, in which, on their retreat towards Washington the Union army of heroes is destroyed in consequence of the total incapacity of their Commanding General; till on the third day of September, they are forced to seek protection in the almost ungarrisoned fortifications constructed by McClellan in front of Washington. The enemy, in close proximity to the National Capital, with Maryland and Pennsylvania at their mercy, is halting to decide in what direction to advance.

The more intelligent the rank and file of an army, the more accomplished ought to be their officers. The better disciplined an army, the more it will suffer in the hands of an incompetent general. Armies experienced in actual warfare, require the most precise orders from their leaders. These are well established military truisms. Pope's deplorable August campaign, fully demonstrates their correctness. The troops under General McDowell had before this campaign hardly seen any active service; the men did not understand to distinguish a judicious movement from a fatal one; they were tumbled about from one place to another, without knowing why nor caring what for.

The troops under Generals Banks and Sigel had seen considerable service under their able commanders, and were well disciplined; they very soon perceived the total want of a proper plan and purpose in, the movements undertaken by General Pope; at the outset they had, relying on competent leadership, executed every movement as ordered and consequently had suffered in a fearful manner; Banks left without any orders at Brestow, when General Pope commenced his retreat, was actually surrounded by the enemy and had to cut his way through to reach Fairfax Court House ; Sigel, who was placed in the advance as long as the army faced the enemy, and had to cover the retreat, when General Pope began to look in the rear,—did not hesitate, it is said, to express his opinion of the total incompetence of that gentleman, and to call to strict account General McDowell, who by the want of General Pope's better judgment was for a time placed in command over Major-General Sigel, while Brigadier-General Reno had an independent command of a corps.*

The generals and troops of the army of the Potomac, gradually all placed under the command of General Pope, had by long experience under General McClellan, learned to understand that every movement of a Division or Corps forms part of a well-digested and completely matured plan of operations, and that the orders for the execution thereof were concise in every respect. These troops under men like Hooker, Heintzleman, Sumner, Fitzjohn Porter, Griffin, Franklin, Kearney and Stephens—every one of them the hero of a hard fought battle—at first went into action under General Pope, with the same cheerfulness that led them victorious through all dangers on the Peninsula, but they very soon found they had a commander without a head and became dissatisfied.

The newspapers, on the 15th day of October, published the following letter, said to have been addressed on the 4th day of August, by

---

*To place General McDowell in battle over General Sigel, is to put the horse upon the rider. If General Pope had not been completely blinded by his self-conceit he would have taken advantage of his good luck to have a man like Sigel in his army ; he would have given to that officer, the de facto command of the army of Virginia, while he and McDowell in the meanwhile might have taken the best possible care of themselves, sent despatches of brilliant victories to Washington and finally might have reaped all the glory. We regret that General Sigel has thought it proper, in time of war, on one or more occasions to make a political speech, but nevertheless we are forced to express our conviction, that of all the officers in the army of Virginia the only one capable to save that army from utter ruin, after the enemies' advance had passed Thoroughfare Gap, is Franz Sigel. In him the advantages of the most thorough military education and extensive experience as a commander are combined, with the rare gift of military genius, unsurpassed bravery, energy, and a bull-dog tenacity. These qualities he displayed in his celebrated retreats from Carthage and from Rolla, as well as at the battle of Pea Ridge, when holding command under a general of inferior capacities, he had to force upon that gentleman a complete victory over the rebel army when a surrender to the latter, was in that strategist's opinion the only chance for him. He displayed those qualities also in the three days' engagements on the Rapidan, after the affair of Cedar Mountains, where with a small corps he successfully disputed the crossing of that river by the rebels till he was ordered to move according to Pope's directions with McDowell.

Major-General Kearney, of the army of the Potomac, to a Mr. Halstead of New Jersey:

HARRISON'S LANDING, August 4, 1862.

DEAR PET—I thank you for your kind, long letter. You extend to me hope. You suggest withdrawing me and my division from this ignoble position. With Pope's army I would breathe again.

We have no generals. McClellan is the failure I ever proclaimed him. He has been punished, just as I at once comprehended the moves of the parties. He will only get us in more follies, more waste of blood, fighting by driblets. He has lost the confidence of all. Nor has he a single officer about him capable of bettering us. Sumnor is a "bull in a china shop," and a sure enough blunderer. ——— lest his corps gratuitously at Fair Oaks. He is not now in his right place, and will be much worse. ——— is a small brain, ossified in a " 4 company" garrison on the frontier. He was not "of us" in Mexico, but in a rear column once saw a distant flash in a guerilla fight. His skill is a myth, a poetical version of his own part at Bull Run. Porter is good in nature, but weak as water—the parent of all this disaster for his want of generalship on the Chickahominy. ——— and Franklin are talented engineers. They might make good generals if they understood the value of elements in their calculations; as it is, they are dangerous failures.

When ——— was drunk he had some few men drowned before Yorktown. I know of no other feat of his. Franklin's battle of West Point was a most runaway picket fight of ours. His part on the Chickahominy was unpardonable. He sent over a division (his own), was present on that side out of fire, and never interfered to protect them from being sacrificed by driblets and rendered a prey to their false position. I was horrified at it, as described by General Taylor and all others. Is it surprising that I want to get out of this mess? Besides, they have sent me a major generalship, like all these others, dated from 4th July, muddled in a batch of new and very ordinary junior officers. Do they forget that I was appointed twelfth on the original list? that I, on the heels of Bull Run, faced the enemy with a Jersey brigade in advance of all others, against all. McClellan, McDowell, *et id omne genus*, nearly forcing me to come back of the "Seminary." Do they forget me at Manassas? My Jersey brigade that infected with panic the retiring enemy? Has Williamsburg never come to their ears? Oh, no! I really feel aggravated beyond endurance. Discipline becomes degradation if not wielded with justice. Patriotism cannot, amid all her sacrifices, claim that of self respect. Generals, victorious in the past, are not called on to expose their troops, unless those brave men are acknowledged. Their identity in their chief's promotion claims a date of their own high acts. Oh, no, I am nearer returning to the home I have given up, to the interests I have sacrificed, to my cherished wife, whose anxiety oppresses me, than I ever dreamt of in a war for the Union. But if the infatuate North are weak enough to let this crisis be managed by "small men of small motives," I am not willing to be their puppet.

My dear Pet, I am too lazy, and too little interested to dive into the future of this " little box of heresies," so do tell me—what do the people at the North look forward to in the future? I fear lest this war will die out in rapid imbecility.

For McClellan, he is burnt out. Never once on a battle field, you have nothing to hope from him as a leader of a column. How do they expect Pope to beat, with a very inferior force, the veterans of Ewell and Jackson? But these are episodes. We deceive ourselves. There was a people of old—it was the warrior Spartan, with his Helot of the fields. The South have realized it. There was an ambitious people of recent times, and a conscription pandered to her invasions. At this moment the South exemplifies them both. " Peace, peace !" but there is no peace. No, not even with a disruptured Union. Let the North cast away that delusion.

Draft we must, or the disciplined thousands of the South will redeem scrip in Philadelphia; and yet the true North must accept it, and quickly, to a man, or the moment it draggles in debate Maryland, Tennessee, and Kentucky will cast past victories to the winds, and rise with their nearly allied rebel kin. My dear Pet, I shall be delighted when Henry can come on. As to Colonel Halstead, I think that his case is a type of the insane and unnecessary despotism introduced into the army under the auspices of McClellan and his very weak aids. It is now too late, but why was not the cavalry put in my charge at the commencement? Two nights ago the rebel batteries fired from across the river, and killed and wounded some thirty men. Last night Hooker started on a crude expedition to Malvern Hills. He went out four miles and came back again. Still, a " false fuss" injures the whole army. McClellan is dangerous, from the want of digesting his plans. He positively has no talents. Adieu. Get me and my " fighting division" with Pope. With best regards, yours
KEARNEY.

This document, dated Harrison's Landing, commences Dear Pet; it speaks of a mutual friend as Henry; shows thereby great intimacy between the writer and the Dear Pet, but it is nevertheless signed very formal—" Kearney"—not your Philip, as everybody would expect from Dear Pet's intimate friend. The writer says, How do they expect Pope to beat, with a very inferior force, the veterans of Ewell and Jackson? How could Kearney know, on the 4th of August, at Harrison's Landing, first, that the army of Virginia, under Pope, was very inferior to the veterans under Ewell and Jackson, when Pope reports he had 32,000 men at Cedar Mountain? and how did he know that either of these generals, or both of them, would have to be fought by Pope? when at that date, five days before the battle of Cedar Mountain, not even General Pope had the least idea of the strength opposed to him, nor of the name of their commander, and does in his report thereof not mention the name of the rebel general? The letter continues: "Peace, peace," but there is no peace. Let the North cast away this delusion. All the rumors of peace propositions, and the talk about peace in the rebel Congress, as well as the peace speculations at the North occurred when the rebel army was in Maryland in the early part of September, after General Kearney had died on the battle-field. The names of several officers alluded to in the letter are omitted, while those of the greater number, and in particular of those most unscrupulously criticised, are written in full.

The letter, in its tendencies condemning everybody except the author; complaining of want of proper appreciation of his superiority over everybody; and requesting the friend to get him more power and into a higher rank; resembles very much the letter addressed to a friend by General Shields, immediately after the battle of Winchester, against Jackson, March 22d, 1862.

For these reasons, we doubt the letter in question to be a genuine one, written by Major-General Kearney.

If, nevertheless, Major-General Kearney has written this identical letter to Mr. Halstead, we think the general must, at the time, have been laboring under partial insanity. According to all we have ever heard of him—we did not know him ourselves—he was a gentleman of education; an officer who had travelled in Europe, and held a commission in the French army with credit to himself and to his country. He had, consequently, occasion to associate with French officers, and become familiar with the rules of strictest propriety governing the conduct of comrades-in-arms towards each other; to learn the utter contempt in which an officer would be held who should express opinions discreditable to any other officer, behind his back, to a third person, and has had occasion to form an opinion of the military qualifications of a general. An officer, possessing these advantages, in his right mind, could never forget himself so far as to write a long epistle, touching on almost all the leading topics of the day, for the sole purpose of defaming the commanding general of the army wherein he holds a command, as well as every general in that army who has ever been mentioned with distinction, glorifying only himself and General Pope. Pope at that time, had never had occasion to show what he could do as the leader of an army, but had written a highly improper proclamation to the army of Virginia, and was known to have been exceedingly erratic in his reports as to the capture by him of a large portion of Beauregard's army on their retreat from Corinth, and as to the occupation of Gordonsville. Nor could his extensive experience have left him, at his time of life, so miserable a judge of the qualifications of a commanding officer, and of his own best interest, as to prefer a command under the unmilitary, self-conceited, in every respect disqualified officer, General Pope has proved himself to be, instead of one under the experienced, gifted, dignified and successful commander of the army of the Potomac, and with his distinguished commanders of corps and of divisions, who had shared with General Kearney the dangers and privations as well as the glory of many a hard-fought battle.

Gen. Pope's report of his campaign, of Sept. 3d, '62, (it does not say where the headquarters of the Army of Virginia are,) is a document in keeping with his proceedings since he was, to his and the country's misfortune, put in command of the Army of Virginia. He tries to convince the General-in-Chief, (who ought to know best what were the objects to be gained by the Army of Virginia, and what instructions he had given to the commander thereof), that he committed this continuous line of military blunders for the purpose of saving the Army of the Potomac from destruction, on the James River; while in all the battles except that on the 9th of August, at Cedar Creek, a smaller or larger part of that army was fighting under his command; while the heaviest fighting was done by these corps, and while the almost complete destruction of the Army of the Potomac, (which counts the gallant Kearney and General Stephens among those thousands who, with their lives, sealed the devotion of that noble army to the Government and the flag of the Union,) is one of the greatest losses the country has had to suffer from Gen. Pope's utter failure as a commander.* He finds fault with Gen. Fitz John Porter, Gen. Griffin and others, and has not a word of thanks for Gen. Sigel, while he insinuates that Gen. McClellan has acted wrong in requesting him to send a proper escort for forage, ammunition and provisions, which he had asked for from the latter. McClellan, as we have mentioned, had no troops left him, but would, according to army regulations, have been held responsible, and justly so, for the careless imprudence of sending government stores over routes everywhere harrassed by the enemy, without proper escort. His orders for the movements of troops are in some instances as unmilitary as those of Gen. McDowell, at Bull Run No. 1.

---

*He censures everybody, either direct or by implication; he complains that others have not directed the movements of the Army of Virginia, in his own department, to positions which he had neglected to occupy; he omits dates, which of course confuses his report; he repeats statements said to have been made to him, while he has to admit that he knew them from his own knowledge to be false; he appeals to his countrymen to judge of his military qualifications.

The management of the Army of Virginia by Pope, and the unpardonable reckless mismanagement of the entire campaign, calls to mind Napoleon's well known opinion in regard to an army of lions commanded by a quadruped distinguished for the length of his ears. At the same time we cannot well fail to see how quick retribution has overtaken the man who, in his first proclamation to the army dared to cast a slur at Gen. McClellan; who boasted he had only seen the backs of the enemy, and who promised his army the inscription of many names of glorious battles upon their colors. His neglect of selecting a strong position, and of protecting his line of retreat, and his policy to order his army to live upon the country and to dispense with means of transportation; in fact his utter ignorance and self-conceit have cost the country thousands of valuable lives, millions of treasure, an entire campaign, have drawn the rebel army across the Potomac into Maryland, and have cheated the gallant soldiers of the honorable reward for all their fatigues, dangers and privations, the inscription on their colors of the name of a new Union victory. In his official report, over his own signature, he is forced to express thanks to the corps of the Army of the Potomac, and he has to declare that he had no chance left him but to retreat or to starve.

A colonel of the army, dangerously wounded, writes a letter to his family, declaring *he was dying a victim to the ignorance of Pope and the treachery of McDowell.* Gen. McDowell took occasion to request the President to order a court of investigation in this matter; this request, in our opinion, ought to have been made to the Commander-in-Chief of the Army, at whose hands it probably would have received proper attention; the President, we apprehend, will not be able to take any notice thereof.

On the day on which the defeated army of Gen. Pope reached the fortifications in front of Washington, he was relieved of his command; not dismissed from the army, but ordered to take command of the department west of the Mississippi.

When the Government at Washington, by the not very distant roar of cannon, and by the appearance of the rebel scouts near the Chain Bridge, was informed that all the reports of brilliant victories, sent in by Gen. Pope, had not arrested the advance of Robert Lee's army to almost within speaking distance of Arlington Heights, and that the chances of his coming still nearer were rather alarming, it seemed a matter of utmost necessity and of personal safety, (even before Gen. Pope would reach Washington, to be deprived of his command,) to find an officer competent to defend the National Capital against occupation by the rebels.

General James S. Wadsworth was, to be sure, still Military Governor of the District of Columbia, and nominally held command of all the fortifications around the city of Washington. He was entitled to the command—*de facto*—and we have no doubt he was ready and eager to assume it, if only to prove that he did not hold a sinecure ; but we have not learned that at this most critical time of Mr. Lincoln's administration General Wadsworth was ever thought of as the man for that command. It is said it was tendered to General Ambrose Burnside, who in declining its acceptance declared General McClellan to be the best qualified man to save the capital, which reply proved Burnside's ambition subordinate to his patriotism, and the General to be a real hero. Other Generals were consulted ; they all pointed to McClellan as the only man for the crisis; General Halleck, invited to attend a cabinet meeting, is said to have been asked how many combinations there were under existing circumstances for the government to decide upon ? to which he replied, there were but two; either to have Stonewall Jackson in Washington or to place McClellan in command of all that was left of the armies, because he alone could stem the rebel advances. Finally the President went to see the man who had just returned from a six months' summer campaign, in a southern climate, who had shared with his soldiers the bodily fatigues, the privations and the dangers of battles, while his brain had been constantly working for the benefit of every man in his command; from a campaign where his success had been prevented by nonfulfillment of promises made him by the Administration. The President had to see the man whom a few days ago he had stripped of his command, the man whom almost that very day, persons in the confidence of the Administration had accused of treasonable intentions. He had to see the man who had been publicly sneered at by the Secretary of War and by General Pope, both of them enjoying the President's confidence; the man who under all these circumstances had never uttered a word of complaint or of retaliation, who had strictly attended to his duties and had left the rest with God. How great that man of small stature must then have appeared to the President!

All that was said during this interview will probably not be made known until the memoirs of General McClellan, one of these days, shall appear in print; because the President can not very well have any reason to make it known and McClellan has proved that he never talks. There can be no doubt that General McClellan, who well knew that no power on earth could *compel* him to resume command after the treatment he had received at the hands of Mr. Lincoln's administration, had promises made him that he should promptly receive for his army all they needed, and that he should hereafter not be interfered with by anybody.

Time alone can show how such promises are carried out while Edward M. Stanton remains Secretary of War.

On the 2d day of September General McClellan was appointed to command the fortifications around Washington, and all the troops for the defence of the Capital, which meant of all that remained of the armies of Virginia, of the Potomac, and Burnside's forces. On the same day McClellan went into Virginia to visit the troops; his very presence electrified and invigorated them; on the 4th of September he issued the following General Order:

GENERAL ORDERS—No. 1.
WASHINGTON, Sept. 4, 1862.

First—Pursuant to General Orders No. 122 from the War Department, Adjutant-General's office, of the 2d inst., the undersigned hereby assumes command of the fortifications of Washington and of all the troops for the defense of the Capital.

Second—The heads of the staff departments of the Army of the Potomac will be in charge of their respective departments at these headquarters.

Third—In addition to the consolidated morning reports required by the circular of this date from these headquarters, reports will be made by corps commanders as to their compliance with the assignment to positions heretofore given them, stating definitely the ground occupied and covered by their commands, and as to what progress has been made in obedience to the orders already issued to place their commands in condition for immediate service.

G. B. McCLELLAN, Major-General.

S. WILLIAMS, Assistant Adjutant-General.

which will bear comparison with the first order of General Pope to the Army of Virginia, on account of the pen and ink portraits it furnishes, of the two men.

The army of the Potomac had suffered great losses during the seven days' battle, which had never been made good. The two weeks' campaign with Pope had greatly reduced its already small numbers, and had cost it many valuable officers; nevertheless Gen. McClellan made this army the nucleus around which to group the corps that were now, for the first time, placed under his command, as well as the new volunteers which had, to some extent, reached Washington. He himself, Burnside, Sigel, Banks, the commanders of corps and of divisions, the chiefs of the various departments of his army, and his entire staff, were at work day and night. The confusion, the disorganization, and the demoralization in which the army had returned to Washington soon disappeared, and discipline, order, and cheerfulness became again the order of the day. Fabulous as it may appear, it is nevertheless true that overcoming all obstacles and difficulties in his way, and infusing his own zeal, determination, and perseverance into every one with whom he came in contact, McClellan succeeded in organizing a proper garrison in the fortifications around Washington, for the safety of the capital, over which he placed General Banks in command; two corps to co-operate with the latter in Virginia, under General Heintzleman and General Sigel; and on the 8th day of September he left Washington with an army of about 65,000 men, to meet General Robert Lee, who had sent one of his corps across the Potomac into Maryland, while he himself, with the bulk of his army, moved up the Cumberland Valley, to cross at Williamsport and Sharpstown.

Before leaving the Capital, General McClellan, whose official district was not definitely specified, but who went wherever danger threatened the country, suggested the propriety of abandoning Harper's Ferry, and fortifying Maryland Heights, which he considered impregnable. General Wool, in whose Department both places lay, was advised with; he communicated with Colonel Miles, commandant of Harper's Ferry, and received the assurance that he would hold the Ferry under all circumstances against any force. McClellan could not do more.

On the 11th September he occupied Barnsville, and took possession of Sugar Loaf Mountain; while Gen. Lee issued on the same day a proclamation to the people of Maryland, calling upon them to join the rebellion. On the 13th of September McClellan entered Frederick City, whence the rebels had made a hasty retreat; on the 15th Hooker and Reno drove the rebels, at the point of the bayonet, from South Mountain, and gained possession of Middletown; in both of which engagements the rebels occupied positions on the top of a mountain ridge, while our men had to attack them up hill. Lee had, in the meantime, sent Jackson to feel Harper's Ferry, and to that General's agreeable surprise, the commander of that place surrendered on Monday 16th, after having not even been asked to do so by the enemy. This act, against which McClellan had cautioned; the President, which could not have been done in better style if Jeff. Davis had appointed and instructed the commandant, gave to Lee's army the benefit of two bridges across the Potomac, of about 12,000 superior rifles, 50 guns, numerous small arms, quantities of ammunition, of stores, of uniforms, and of equipments of all kinds; deprived the Union army of over 10,000 fighting men, and added to Lee's available force all the men otherwise required to take care of Harper's Ferry. It further prevented McClellan from advancing his army above Harper's Ferry, and deprived him of the only bridge across the river that could have been of advantage to him. Lee concentrated his forces, to prevent the passage of Antietam Creek by the Union army; McClellan considered the point of sufficient importance, and the time about as good as any other for a fight. On the 17th of September, the Rebel army and the Union army, for the first time during the war, stood arrayed against each other in regular line of battle, with a front about four miles in length. For the first time did the topography of the country present an opportunity to the commanding Generals to have an almost unobstructed view of both the hostile armies. This circumstance necessitated a management of the armies entirely different from that in all the previous important contests during this rebellion. Every strategical error, every tactical imperfection or hesitation, was at once perceived and taken advantage of by the opposite party. The personal influence of the commanding generals became for the first time during this war instantaneously perceptible on every point of the battle-field. The generals in chief command knew that in every movement, in every new combination, everywhere on the field, they met the intellect, the skill, the talent, of their opponent, personified in tens of thousands of living chess-men. On the rebel side, Stonewall Jackson, Ewell, Longstreet, Hill, and others commanded the various corps, under the supreme command of Robert Lee.

Burnside and Porter on the left, Hooker and Franklin on the right; Sumner, Mansfield, Reno, and Richardson, between them, and Pleasonton, in reserve, held the principal commands under McClellan. Lee's army consisted of experienced soldiers, who had fought their way into this battle field from the interior of Rebeldom. McClellan's army had, only three week's ago, under a leader unworthy to command such men, suffered a fearful defeat at the hands of their opponents, had lost many of their best officers, and was to the greater part made up of raw recruits, who had never been under fire. Nevertheless the Union army opened the ball early in the morning with artillery on the right, and gradually all the corps became engaged.

A battle commenced which lasted all the day, in which the most stubborn resistance on the part of the rebels, was overcome with cold steel in the hands of Union soldiers, with strong arms and enduring muscles. Heroic deeds by the officers and men on both sides, call for the admiration of the world, while it curses the fanatic demagogues who have brought about and who now foster this unjustifiable war between brothers. The armies moved to and fro, and the line of battle shaped itself into that of a serpentine, changing frequently the convex to the concave, and *vice versa*. The passage of Antietam Bridge, work laid out for the noble Burnside, was hotly contested by Lee, who at once discovered the importance of the point, and by the assistance of his three bridges across the river, moved immense forces on his right; but all in vain, again and again the Union soldiers would return to the charge, till finally they triumphed, and the bridge was taken and retained, although we are positively assured that Burnside's corps was out of ammunition the last half hour of the fight. Darkness found McClellan in the position occupied by Lee in the morning. Lee was driven about two miles back; both armies equally exhausted, rested on their arms, On the 18th, neither of the combatants felt inclined to renew the battle. On the 19th, when McClellan, who had been reinforced during the night, advanced, he found the rebel army in full retreat across the Potomac, at Harper's Ferry, Sheppardstown, and Williamsport, leaving all their dead, most of their wounded, and a great many stragglers behind. Harper's Ferry was also evacuated by the rebels after they had destroyed the bridges, and was taken possession of by our troops. Thus, fifteen days after he had taken command of a demoralized and defeated army, and ten days after he had left Washington, McClellan, with the gallant officers and men under his command, had driven the rebel army out of Maryland, and saved Pennsylvania from invasion; had fought three battles, the last of them the greatest and the most important ever fought on this continent, against the Commander-in-Chief of the rebel army, an officer of acknowledged ability, assisted by Stonewall Jackson, by Longstreet, by Hill, and by Ewell. These names have been connected with almost every battle in the East. A more brilliant campaign is not recorded in history. The same man who last winter used the spade to construct fortifications, which last summer saved the National Capital; who carefully organized, disciplined and militarized the army of the Potomac, which by its efficacy to day gives the country the benefit of the care and devotion bestowed upon them by their commanders; who secured his position on the Chickahominy by earthworks, which enabled him to defeat the gigantic combinations of the rebel leaders for his destruction; who, with the utmost precaution and without the loss of a single man, moved his entire army from Harrison's Landing to Alexandria; this same man, in his ten days campaign in Maryland, displays a rapidity, a boldness, a dash, unsurpassed by any chieftain. The Governor of Pennsylvania had called out the militia and moved them to the exposed frontier of that State, which movement had undoubtedly its influence upon the rebel armies.

The loss of both armies engaged in Maryland was enormous : the rebel General Garland was killed, and the total number of killed, wounded and prisoners in Lee's army is probably near 25,000, while the Union has to mourn the loss of the distinguished Generals Mansfield and Reno among the killed; the gallant Hooker, Weber and Hatch among the wounded, and in round numbers probably 12,000 killed and put *hors du combat*. That General Lee retreated immediately after the battle of Antietam, proves him to be a General of great foresight. Knowing better than anybody else the exhausted state of his army and being able to form a correct opinion of the condition of the Union army, he at once estimated the advantage under which he could recross the Potomac, with his army divided in small commands, availing themselves of every ford that could be found, if not harrassed by the Union army, and protected in case of an assault from cavalry and a few pieces of artillery by his corps at Harper's Ferry, at Shepherdstown and at Williamsport. He saw how much more orderly his army could move and how much smaller the loss in stragglers and wounded would be, than if awaiting a renewal of the battle, the result of which, in all probability could not be different from that just fought; he would have to retreat, pressed by McClellan, and to recross the river in concentrated masses, therefore with greater danger, and most likely harrassed by the long range Union guns. He therefore improving the chance of a very rainy and very foggy night, commenced his retrogade movement at once, and succeeded in reaching the Virginia shore; he then withdrew his reserves from the three principal crossing places above mentioned, destroyed the bridges and placed the Potomac between himself and the Union army.

The reasons which induced McClellan not to renew the battle on the 18th are stronger even than those that governed Lee in his decision to retreat. The Union army in all its corps had had a very hard day's work, which in particular told upon the new troops; it was almost entirely out of ammunition; by the extreme efforts only of officers and men the rebels had been forced to retreat. To lead these same troops (he had no others), into battle again before they were fully rested, would have induced so skillful a General as Robert Lee to slowly fall back, to draw McClellan with his fatigued troops after him, till he had placed his own army under the protection of Maryland Heights. From this strong position his artillery would have caused fearful havoc in the Union army, while the best rebel troops would have been selected, allowed a few hours rest and refreshments, after which they would have been led to attack McClellan, and in all probability with success; because desperate positions call forth the most powerful exertions of men. Upon this truth is based the old strategic maxim: "build golden bridges for a retreating enemy." Why did McClellan not follow Lee across the river when on the 19th and 20th he had rested his army and had received reinforcements? He could not do it, because he and the Government had not troops enough to do it with, and the latter has not yet been able to make good the great losses in shoes, uniforms and ammunition, suffered by the army during the lamentable campaign under General Pope. To cross the Potomac without bridges, in the face of Lee's batteries on the opposite shore, is an entirely different affair from that performed by the rebel army, who had all the bridges across and both sides of the river in their possession. Had the government had troops, General Halleck would have sent Sigel, who is always ready, with 20,000 men on the Virginia side to Harper's Ferry to destroy the bridges before Lee could use them, and thereby to place the rebel army between two fires. The call for 300,000 volunteers was made in July instead of March, 1862, when it ought to have been. The most urgent appeals from all quarters to send volunteers to fill up the ranks of the old, instead of raising new regiments, met with no hearty response from the State governments. Generals Sickles and Meagher truly said, the process is too slow by which a citizen is transformed into a soldier. To organise new regiments, under inexperienced officers, requires more time than the country at this crisis could spare; the country, as well as Generals Halleck, McClellan and Sigel, have for the present to rest content with what has been achieved in September last.

The withdrawal of the Pennsylvania militia, the moment the enemy was out of sight, shows the want of co-operation between the State and United States Governments. The unprotected condition of the Potomac, above and below the position occupied by the army under McClellan, we have to put down as another evidence that neither Gen. Halleck nor Gen. Wool had any troops to protect the river. That Gen. Lee sent only a cavalry raid into Pennsylvania, instead of taking his entire army there, we consider the strongest evidence of their crippled condition. He might be forced to a hasty retreat, or could be badly cut up in battle, if the corps under Gens. Heintzelman and Sigel, in Virginia, and the army under McClellan, in Maryland, were in a perfect state of efficiency. As it is, Sigel has to wait for horses to mount his cavalry, and McClellan for other necessaries for his troops, and the country has to be patient.

But how is it possible that the advance of the Union armies has to be delayed for want of proper equipment, armament or ammunition; while the rebels, who are cut off from the entire world by our effective blockade, who have no large boot, shoe and other factories, such as the North, and Massachusetts in particular, can justly boast of, can and do move their large armies speedily, and always prepared, from battle field to battle field?

Probably because the utterly despotic government of Jefferson Davis is forced to concentrate all its energies, first and foremost, for the purpose of keeping up the highest possible state of efficiency in the rebel army, upon which alone depends the existence of that Government and the success of their rebellious intentions, and further because the Confederates own all the slaves, and therefore do not trouble themselves about the slavery question.

The smoke of the battle of Antietam had hardly cleared off, the slain had not all been buried, and the wounded had not all yet been cared for, when on the 22d of September, President Lincoln issued the most important document that ever emanated from any President of these United States—his Proclamation abolishing Slavery in all the Southern States that on the first day of January next shall be in rebellion.

The proclamation, at that moment, took the country by surprise; the people anxiously waited to learn that man's opinion about this document, who but a few days ago had saved the Capital and probably the Administration of his country. He took his own time to consider a subject of so immeasurable importance for good or for evil to the civilized world.

On the 7th day of October, General McClellan issued the following order to the army under his command:

GENERAL ORDERS—NO. 163.

HEADQUARTERS, ARMY OF THE POTOMAC,
CAMP NEAR SHARPSBURG, Md., Oct. 7, 1862.

The attention of the officers and soldiers of the Army of the Potomac is called to General Orders No. 130, War Department, Sept. 24, 1862, publishing to the army the President's proclamation of Sept. 22.

A proclamation of such grave moment to the nation, officially communicated to the army, affords to the General commanding an opportunity of defining specifically to the officers and soldiers under his command the relation borne by all persons in the military service of the United States towards the civil authorities of the Government. The constitution confides to the civil authorities, legislative, judicial, and executive, the power and duty of making, expounding, and executing the federal laws. Armed forces are raised and supported simply to sustain the civil authorities, and are to be held in strict subordination thereto in all respects. This fundamental rule of our political system is essential to the security of our republican institutions, and should be thoroughly understood and observed by every soldier. The principle upon which, and the objects for which, armies shall be employed in suppressing the rebellion, must be determined and declared by the civil authorities, and the chief Executive, who is charged with the administration of the national affairs, is the proper and only source through which the views and orders of the Government can be made known to the armies of the nation.

Discussion by officers and soldiers concerning public measures determined upon and declared by the Government, when carried at all beyond the ordinary temperate and respectful expression of opinion, tend greatly to impair and destroy the discipline and efficiency of troops by substituting the spirit of political faction for that firm, steady, and earnest support of the authority of the Government which is the highest duty of the American soldier. The remedy for political errors, if any are committed, is to be found only in the action of the people at the polls.

In thus calling the attention of the army to the true relation between the soldiers and the Government, the General commanding merely adverts to an evil against which it has been thought advisable during our whole history to guard the armies of the Republic, and in so doing he will not be considered by any right minded person as casting any reflection upon that loyalty and good conduct which has been so fully illustrated upon so many battle fields. In carrying out all measures of public policy this army will, of course, be guided by the same rules of mercy and Christianity that have ever controlled its conduct towards the defenceless.

By command of

Major-General McCLELLAN.

JAMES A. HARDEE, Lieutenant-Colonel, Aid-de-Camp, and Acting Assistant Adjutant General.

This order relieved the anxiety of the people, because it conveys the redeeming assurance that the almost universal corruption, threatening the ruin of the country, has left us at least one man; a soldier unsurpassed by the most famous of any age; adored by an army composed of his fellow citizens; the hero of some of the greatest battles ever fought—who, ill treated in the most unwarrantable manner by the Administration, at the very moment when corrupt officials allow his army to suffer from want of the indispensable necessaries, and prevent him from following up his successes in the field — while people unacquainted with this fact complain of his inactivity — tells those tens of thousands under his command, and shows by his own acts, that he holds obedience to the constitutional laws of his country to be the first and most sacred duty of the soldier as of the citizen in a Republic, and who thereby proves himself "a patriot."

F. A. P.

NEW YORK, October 25, 1862.

PRICE, 25 CENTS.

MILITARY REVIEW

OF THE

CAMPAIGN IN VIRGINIA & MARYLAND

UNDER

GENERALS J. C. FREMONT, N. P. BANKS, IRWIN McDOWELL,
FRANZ SIGEL, JOHN POPE, JAMES S. WADSWORTH,
WM. H. HALLECK, GEORGE B. McCLELLAN,
AND AMBROSE BURNSIDE.

In 1862,

BY

FRED'K A. PETERSEN.

PART II.

---

*He that is truly dedicated to war
Hath no self-love; nor he that loves himself
Hath not essentially, but by circumstances,
The name of valor.*
— SHAKSPEARE.

𝔄 Contribution to the Future History of the United States.

NEW-YORK:

WHOLESALE AGENTS: { SINCLAIR TOUSEY, 121 NASSAU STREET,
{ H. DEXTER, 113 NASSAU STREET.

Entered according to Act of Congress in the year 1862, by F. A. Petersen, in the Clerk's Office of the District Court of the Southern District of New-York.

MILITARY REVIEW

OF THE

CAMPAIGN IN VIRGINIA & MARYLAND

In 1862.

PART II.

"Time alone can show how such promises will be carried out while Edwin M. Stanton remains Secretary of War." We said in October last* speaking of the promises made to General McClellan by President Lincoln on the first day of September last, when he declared the country the government and the army to be lost, unless the General would apply his genius and skill as a commander, and his irresistible influence over our soldiers to the reorganization of the army, which, demoralized under Mr. Stanton and General Halleck from April to August, had, under General Pope been disastrously defeated, and had been driven behind the fortifications near Washington; and then, with the reorganised army to protect the Capital from occupation by the rebels, and to save that Administration which had prevented the success of his campaign in the Peninsula.

The ink with which the above statement was written, had scarcely dried, when events demonstrated that the fulfilment of the promises made by our President ceased as soon as the capital and the cabinet were not any longer in imminent danger, and that plots and machinations against McClellan commenced anew and with increased boldness.

We beg the reader will remember the following facts. Large quantities of provisions, forage, equipments and ammunition, on their return from Harrison's Landing, by the army of the Potomac, stored

* Page 47 Part 1st.

at Aquia Creek, and by the army under General McDowell taken to Fredericksburg, had to be destroyed by our own troops to prevent the enemy from getting them, at the time when both places were suddenly abandoned in consequence of the disastrous defeat of all the brave troops, in July and August last, entrusted to the command of General Pope. Also that the visit paid by the rebels to General Pope's headquarters at Catlett's Station caused great loss of subsistence, equipments and ammunition of every kind; also that all which had not been destroyed or lost already, was taken from him during the the last five days in August, when Lee drove General Pope rapidly and with fearful losses from Thoroughfare Gap to the fortifications near Washington; that this very large quantity of subsistence, equipments and ammunition was lost in the short space of little over two weeks; that the long and forced marches and counter-marches of the corps under General Pope had caused unusual wear and tear in their equipments of every kind.

It will further be remembered that Gen. McClellan and his reorganized army left Washington for the Maryland campaign only *one week* after General Pope's retreating army had found shelter behind the fortifications near the city, and that consequently the government had very little time to replace the enormous losses of every description;—that the Maryland Campaign, in consequence of the extraordinary rapidity of movements, and the quick succession of it's battles, had consumed in equipments and in ammunition, all that the Government might have furnished during that one week in Washington. That McClellan's army on its march from Frederick City to South Mountain and Antietam Creek, had to abandon the railroad line, whereby the transportation of new supplies was of necessity retarded.

It is natural that in consequence of all these circumstances, and in consequence of the fierceness and long duration of the great battle of Antietam, the army of the Potomac, after it had followed Lee to the left bank of the Potomac, should stand sorely in need of shoes, uniforms, ammunition, arms, and of materials of every kind. The fact is large numbers of soldiers had to go barefooted because they had no shoes. That such was the actual condition of the army, McClellan represented to the Government, and the nation at large was by the thousand means of communication between the army and the people, in every section of the country, fully aware of the fact.

Deeply deploring the imbecile management of the War Department, which had placed the army of the most liberal nation in such a condition, the people expected the Government to make every possible exertion, to place the army of the Potomac, in the shortest possible time, in condition to open a new campaign.

The same evil spirits, however, who by their "*on to Richmond*" caused the disgraceful "Bull Run," the same who in March last induced the president to relieve McClellan from the command as General-in-Chief of the army; who thereby deprived the country of the services of the General best qualified for that office, and caused our failure in suppressing the rebellion—the same evil spirits who in August last made the President degrade McClellan and deprive him of his command—the same who cowed down when Lee's army stood in front of Washington, and when personal danger made Mr. Lincoln discard the opinion of his irresponsible advisers and reinstate McClellan—these same evil spirits circulated rumors about the inactivity of the army of the Potomac; about the loss of the favorable season for a fall campaign; about McClellan's disinclination to pursue or to fight Lee; about the exaggeration of the wants of the army, *et cetera.*

The people, that is a large majority of them, had too much common sense to doubt the General, who, during the entire war, has proved himself a self-sacrificing patriotic soldier. A few, however, bound to prevent this war from being brought to a satisfactory termination by McClellan, based upon the above-stated rumors their new plans against him.

The fearful losses from June to September sustained by the armies of the Potomac and by those other corps that by degrees had been attached to it, amounting in the aggregate to not less than 100,000 men—the loss of many of the best officers—the incorporation of new volunteer regiments, under inexperienced officers—all this forced upon General McClellan the duty, to properly reorganize, discipline and strengthen his army, to fill up the thinned ranks of the old regiments, and to prepare the new ones for actual service. At the same time he had to guard the, (at this season in many places fordable) Potomac; and he had to impress the rebel General Lee with the apprehension that at any moment he would be attacked by the army of the Potomac.

In September, when he accepted the command of all the troops concentrated in Virginia, the President expressly placed Gen. McClellan above the official interference of Messrs. Stanton and Halleck, and it was therefore, also McClellan's duty, aside from all the above specified business, to devise a plan for the new campaign.

The campaign in Maryland was at an end; and there can be but one opinion among military men, that this war will never be brought to a satisfactory end, and that the rebellion can never be conquered, if the Union armies follow, in whatever direction the commanders of the rebels may draw them. To destroy the rebel army we have to compel their generals to meet us, and accept battle wherever the strategical combinations of our generals shall designate the field of operations. In our opinion there exists only one strategical combination.

To defeat the rebel army in Virginia General McClellan had to increase and in every manner to perfect his army as rapidly as possible under all circumstances, before the Potomac should rise high enough to make all the fords impracticable; to have collected, somewhere on the Potomac, say at Alexandria, the largest possible number of transports; to direct a great many of the new volunteer regiments toward his position on the Upper Potomac, for the purpose of occupying the front when and where vacated by the efficient old regiments sent to Alexandria for embarkation; to direct frequent and strong reconnoisances against the enemy's position on the right bank of the Potomac, for the purpose of strengthening their apprehension of an impending attack *en masse*. Whenever the river shall have risen to high water mark, that it can be crossed only on bridges, which the enemy does not possess, then to float down the Potomac from Alexandria as large and as efficient an army as can be carried, accompanied by the pontoon trains and by some half-a-dozen iron gunboats; to ascend the James river to a point as near fort Darling as practicable; there disembark, and thence move on Richmond. The new regiments on the upper Potomac to be left there, to screen the withdrawal of the main army, and by their presence to keep General Lee as long as possible in front of them, on the opposite shore; eventually these new regiments to form a reserve corps for coöperation with the army when and where needed. To direct the army at and near Suffolk, to advance towards Petersburg, and thereby to coöperate with the army of the Potomac.

We consider this the only sound and effective strategical combination that under all the existing circumstances General McClellan could entertain. Here are our reasons:

It cannot be doubted that, if Gen. McClellan's plan for his Peninsular campaign had not been betrayed to the rebel General Johnson, before its execution had commenced, the army of the Potomac would have taken Richmond in May last, and that thereby the back-bone of the rebellion would have been broken. Even after Johnson, with his army, had reached Richmond from Manassas, the rebel capital would have been in possession of the army of the Potomac, before the rebel reinforcement from the West could have reached it, had not the President and Mr. Stanton, by their meddling with matters of which they are profoundly ignorant, prevented the execution of McClellan's plan, in depriving him, as soon as he himself had embarked for the Peninsula, of the largest corps of his entire army, as proved by the evidence in the McDowell court of enquiry.

In March, as well as in October last, the main rebel army was threatening Washington, but the fortifications protecting the capital were more perfect and stronger in October than they had been last spring. In March the defence of these fortifications had to be entrusted to James S. Wadsworth, a politician; while in October, Heintzelman and Sigel, both of them experienced and tried Generals, had command of these fortifications and the troops cooperating for the protection of the capital. Their forces could be rapidly increased by the daily reporting new volunteer regiments, organized under the President's call for 600,000 men.

Moving to the Peninsula last spring, the army of the Potomac instantaneously drew the rebel army away from Manassas to Richmond, and thereby liberated Virginia, to the Rappahannock, from rebel forces.‡ Returning to the Potomac, it was followed, by the same army, to the gates of Washington. The same cause would have produced the same effect in October or November. The fortifications near Fort Darling and around Richmond, probably have been materially strengthened and extended since August last, when the army of the Potomac was withdrawn from Harrison's Landing, by a strategical blunderer, who had his eyes wide open, but did not see, and who had the ruinous consequences of his evil designs plainly foretold him, but heeded them not.

The Merrimac's blockade of the James River compelled the army of the Potomac to operate against Richmond from the York river After the destruction of the Merrimac by her commander, the Mon-

---

‡Washington was never safer than while the army of the Potomac was at the Peninsula. Strategical blockheads only, could consider the raid in the Shenandoah Valley of 15,000 men under Stonewall Jackson, as directed against the capital, surrounded with strongly garrisoned fortifications. General Lee's instructions to Jackson have shown that it was intended to prevent the corps of General McDowell from being sent to Hanover Court House, there to join our army of the Potomac. The result proves that Robert knows how to play "soldier" with Master Lincoln, and with Master Stanton.

itor, Galena, and Naugatuck unsuccessfully attacked Fort Darling, but there was no army on land to coöperate with them. Afterwards, when the army of the Potomac had moved to the James river, the gunboats were not in condition to renew the attack. In November last several Monitors and other iron gunboats could have attacked the river front, while the army simultaneously would have attacked it by land, and we have no doubt would have taken it. The gunboats thereby would have been enabled to continue their coöperation against Richmond with the armies on both banks of the river.

Active operations of our armies and of our river fleet in the West, facilitated by the rise of the rivers, would have held and occupied the rebel forces there, and would have prevented their concentration near Richmond, so dangerous to the army of the Potomac last summer.

Simultaneous naval demonstrations against Mobile, Charleston and Savannah would have detained a considerable portion of the rebel armies at those ports, and thereby would have contributed to the success of the campaign.

The large number of transports required to float the army of the Potomac from Alexandria to the James river, it is true, might have considerably delayed or perhaps entirely prevented the sailing of the expedition under General Banks; but we firmly believe that the occupation of Richmond by our army, and as a necessary *prelude* thereto, a decisive defeat of the army under General Lee, would have been a more destructive blow to the rebellion, and would constitute a more comprehensive and effective protest against the hostile intentions of the governments in Europe, than any achievement reasonably to be expected by General Banks, at any point of rebeldom can ever produce.

That no other combination can accomplish the object in view, will be admitted when we consider that the army of the Potomac, crossing the river while it is yet low and fordable above Harpers' Ferry, to follow General Lee in the Shenandoah Valley, will have to leave not less than 30,000 men on the left bank for the protection of Maryland, Pennsylvania, and thereby loses so much of its effective strength. When it reaches Winchester it will find Lee's army between that place and Washington, certainly a very undesirable position for an army that depends for its entire subsistence upon the latter city. This relative position of the two armies on the movement down the valley continues to Front Royal; the various gaps in the "Blue Ridge" offer to the rebels facilities to pass to the south side of the said ridge and to mask such a movement by a comparatively insignificant force.

Apart from these geographical and topographical disadvantages to the Union army, Lee is in the valley, master of the situation; he can wait for us, and only accept battle on a field, or in the mountain passes of his own choice. In case the army of the Potomac is victorious in a battle, the result will be simply a loss of men and material with many subsequent battles farther down the valley, in all of which the rebels would have the choice of position. The further the army of the Potomac pursues him, the greater becomes the insecurity of its communication with Harper's Ferry, the base of its operations. The idea that General Sigel or General Heintzelman could move through Manassas Gap and cut off Lee's line of retreat, is untenable. Lee is informed of all the movements of our armies in Virginia; he will move one of his corps through one or more of the gaps, and so get between Washington and both the Union armies; placing Sigel between two fires while the army of the Potomac is held in check in the mountain passes. If the Union armies succeed in escaping all these dangers with moderate loss, and force Lee to retreat beyond Front Royal towards Staunton, they are all the time moving away from their base of operations, and it becomes more and more difficult for them to subside, while the rebel army is steadily approaching their own base of operations and their strongly defended position near Gordonsville. Here they will stand a long siege with comparatively trifling loss, and whenever they conclude to fall back, the destruction of a single bridge in the railroad, will bring the army of the Potomac to a new halt, and all the dangers of this line to Richmond, per Fredericksburg, (alluded to on page 37, 38, part 1st,) will, on the Gordonsville line, threaten the destruction of that army.

If the army of the Potomac crosses the low and fordable river, below Harper's Ferry—after Lee has moved to Winchester—the 30,000 men for the protection of Maryland and Pennsylvania have also to be left on the left bank, and another considerable force has to be moved to Charlestown to protect Harper's Ferry and its approaches. Moving down on the south side of the *Blue Ridge* the army has to take possession and hold in strength all the numerous gaps from Gregories to Manassas—an accomplishment requiring rapidity of movement and good luck, because every one of these gaps, when in possession of the rebel army, will afford General Lee an opportunity to move his force through it to the south side of the ridge, divide the army of the Potomac, and in all probability cause them great losses. The turnpike running parallel with the Blue Ridge in the valley of the Shenandoah, facilitates the concentration of his army at any point, while the want of a parallel road on the south side of the ridge, prevents a speedy concentration of the Union army. In case the army of the Potomac succeeds to get possession and to hold all the passes above mentioned, the march of Lee's army on the turnpike north of the ridge will be easy and rapid, compared with the march of the army of the Potomac over the cross-roads south of the ridge. The rebels will comfortably reach the Robertson River and their previously mentioned position near Gordonsville, before the army of the Potomac can come up with them.

It is true, on this second line of operations, the army of the Potomac is always nearer to Washington than the rebel army; its line of communication is not threatened so much as the line in the valley; but on the other hand it can only march along side and after the rebel army, without a chance to fight a battle before the enemy has reached its stronghold.

In the execution of either one of the two last mentioned combinations, the army of the Potomac, on its approach to Culpepper Court House and vicinity, will have to be concentrated, and all the forces left on the various gaps will have to be recalled, because it is ridiculous to suppose that a line from Harper's Ferry to Thornton Gap, Sperryville, Woodville, Culpepper and Acquia Creek, that is a line of more than 120 miles in length can be properly held and protected against rebel invasion.

The country south and east of the line above indicated, and northwest of the Potomac will, therefore, in all three possible combinations for a new campaign, be unprotected, and will be subject to more or less frequent occupation by the rebels; but when the rebel army follows the army of the Potomac to the peninsula, General Lee will hardly leave any of his men east of Gordonsville, to molest the inhabitants in the district above designated.

To march the army of the Potomac at this late season of the year, poorly equipped, from their position above Harper's Ferry on either one of the last described two lines towards Gordonsville, will involve an amount of hardship, privations and suffering, particularly to the new regiments, which the impossibility of gaining any military advantage should prevent from being inflicted upon those brave heroic soldiers.

General Pleasanton's skirmish near Martinsburg, October 1st, the successful raid to Leesburg, and the capture of a rebel wagon train, and of General Longstreet's official papers by Colonel Egan. October 5;

and several similar reconnoissances to the right bank of the Potomac, we naturally considered as indicative that General McClellan was preparing the execution of the strategical combination which we are firmly convinced to be the only sound one for the new campaign.

In the latter part of October, the army of the Potomac crossed the river and rapidly moved up to and took possession of the several gaps on the south side of the Blue Ridge. Grave doubts, we must confess, then arose in our mind as to the strategical capacity of General McClellan.

The report presented by this Commission, consisting of Major-General Hunter as President, and four other General and Staff Officers of Volunteers, to investigate the conduct of certain officers in connection with the surrender of Harper's Ferry in September last, confirming in substance what we said about the surrender of that position reads thus:

"*The Commission has remarked freely on Colonel Miles, an old officer, who has been killed in the service of his country, and it can not, from any motives of delicacy, refrain from censuring those in high command, when it thinks such censure deserved. The General-in-Chief has testified that General McClellan, after having received orders to repel the enemy invading the State of Maryland, marched only six miles per day, on an average, when pursuing this invading enemy. The General-in-Chief also testifies that in his opinion, he could and should have relieved and protected Harper's Ferry, and in this opinion the Commission fully concur.*"

"*By reference to the evidence it will be seen that at this very moment Colonel Ford abandoned Maryland Heights, his little army was in reality relieved by General Franklin's and Sumner's corps at Crampton's Gap, within seven miles of his position.*"

When we remind the reader of the fact, that the corps of Generals Franklin and Sumner belong to the Army of the Potomac, and acted under command of General McClellan, he will at once see that the Commission contradict themselves; in the last sentence of the first citation they intend to censure McClellan because he could and should have relieved Harper's Ferry; and in the latter citation, they say that Generals Franklin and Sumner—that is, General McClellan— actually had relieved Colonel Ford's little army. The latter assertion is based upon *actual facts;* the previous one based upon the *opinion* of the General-in-Chief—H. W. Halleck.

It is well known that General Halleck was not with McClellan's army in Maryland, nor was he at or near Harper's Ferry; he therefore could not give evidence as an eye-witness, from his own personal knowledge of facts. As an expert he cannot very well have given an opinion, because in that character he does not possess one. General Halleck never in his life had to defend a besieged place, wherein he was relieved; he never led a command to the relief of a besieged brother officer; he never besieged a place held by an armed enemy—his investments having all been of a pacific character, and upon convertible security; consequently in matters of siege and relief he cannot speak from experience. As to General Halleck's superior judgment on military and strategical matters in general, and as to the respect to which his opinion is entitled on that account, we shall take occasion to say a few words on another page.

We cannot understand why the Commission—by the *shameful imbecility* of an *old* officer who *disgracefully surrendered* a strong position; forced to remark freely on that *old* officer, should commit themselves, on General Halleck's *opinion*, to censure General McClellan; who, although a *young* officer, had just accomplished what General Halleck had utterly despaired of (to save the capital, the administration, and General Halleck himself)—when the *evidence of facts*, elicited by themselves, compels them to contradict that opinion in substance. In our opinion it was the duty of the Commission to censure the person high in office who appointed the *old imbecile* officer to the command of an important strategical position, and also him who did not carry out General McClellan's suggestion to permit Miles with all his force to join the Army of the Potomac.

Colonel Miles, as General Wool says (whom the Commission had to admit they erroneously censured), was appointed to the command of Harper's Ferry by Mr. Edwin M. Stanton, and by him, per special order, relieved from the control of any other officer, so that he had to report direct to the Secretary of War. This order has never been repealed. The remark, in General Halleck's Report to the Secretary of War, Dec. 2d., that he "*directed* McClellan *to assume control of all troops within his reach, without regard to departmental lines,*" can evidently be intended only to throw the responsibility for the Harper's Ferry affair upon McClellan; it is not accompanied with the candid statement that the command at Harper's Ferry was *distinctly excluded* by General Halleck's superior, the Secretary of War, from departmental control. That this was the case, that General Halleck was cognizant of it—and that General McClellan understood it to be so—and that the insinuations in the Report of the *General-in-chief of the Army of the United States* to the *Honorable Secretary of War* are false—that the General-in-Chief knew them to be false—and that Mr. Stanton must, of necessity, have known them to be false, because by him Colonel Miles had been removed from the control of General Wool and thereby from General McClellan—all this is established by the witness Halleck, before the Harper's Ferry Commission, who there testifies that on the 11th of September, three days before the battle of South Mountain, General McClellan telegraphed to him "*to give permission to Colonel Miles and his command to join the Army of the Potomac.*" If McClellan had possessed authority to give orders to the commander of Harper's Ferry, as General Halleck insinuates in his report he did have, there would have been no necessity to ask somebody to give permission to Colonel Miles. The General-in-Chief's want of any strategical idea prevented him from comprehending the wisdom of McClellan's suggestion on this as on a previous occasion. As an excuse for this, he says in his report, Dec. 2, "*To withdraw him (Miles) entirely from that position, would not only expose the garrison to capture, but all the stores and artillery collected at that place must either be destroyed or left to the enemy.*" That the garrison *could* have joined McClellan on the 11th is proved by the fact that some 1,500 men left Harper's Ferry on the 14th, the day previous to the surrender, and reached the Army of the Potomac; the stores and artillery actually fell into the enemy's hand by the surrender, before any damage whatever had been done to them; but in addition to this, the arms of 11,000 soldiers fell into the enemy's hands; the Army of the Potomac was deprived of the assistance of that force, and the nation was insulted by a surrender, in the fact that the besieger did not even ask for it, so disgraceful that it exceeds anything recorded in history.

The Commission knew, by official documents at their control, when General McClellan left Washington for Maryland, and when his two corps of Sumner and Franklin were at Crampton Gap. The maps at their control gave them the distance performed by the army, and the Committee themselves could with the same mathematical accuracy as General Halleck for them, ascertain the average number of miles per day marched by the army under McClellan. General Halleck only, we think, could testify that prior to the battle of Antietam*—to that time alone his testimony refers; McClellan was *pursuing* Lee's army. That army was not retreating before nor avoiding the army under McClellan—such a movement alone could enable the latter to *pursue* him; while on the other hand it would make it impossible to *repel* him; what Mr. Halleck testifies McClellan was ordered to do —and what all the world knows he actually did do.

---

* Harper's Ferry was surrendered Sept. 15; the battle of Antietam took place Sept. 17, 1862.

General Lee, when he heard of the approach of Union troops, selected a position on his road to Annapolis Junction, there to fight and to annihilate whatever small force of our army might put themselves in his way. That the demoralized army of General Pope—which he had, only a few days ago, driven before him to Washington—could be reorganized and moved to Maryland in time to dispute his advance, Lee considered an utter impossibility. So strong was he impressed with this, that he detached large forces of his army to Harper's Ferry and to Maryland Heights (who, the moment he found McClellan with his army before him, as the Commission states, were *hurried to the support of Lee*); and that from Frederick City, Sept. 11th, he issued his proclamation to the people of Maryland. The *witness Halleck* was very erratic when he testified that McClellan was *pursuing* the enemy.

After the logic of events had compelled the so-called military heads in Washington—Mr. Stanton, Mr. Halleck, and his other most bitter enemies and unscrupulous slanderers included—either openly to express their conviction, or silently to admit, that if it could be accomplished at all, McClellan was the only man capable to repel the victorious rebel army on their march north; after—under the pressure of this universal and unhesitatingly expressed conviction—Mr. Lincoln had solicited him to assume supreme command of all that was left of the several armies destroyed under Mr. Pope; after that, we say, it seems preposterous to doubt that McClellan was the best judge of the rapidity with which his new regiments could move; of how much time it required to discipline and militarize them on the march; how rapid, under the known mismanagement of the departments in Washington, his ammunition and subsistence trains would come forward; in fine, when and what distance, with the immeasurable responsibilities piled upon his shoulders, he could advance.

For a person in General Halleck's peculiar position—after McClellan has succeeded in repelling the dangerous enemy, thereby saving among others the General himself—to step upon the witness-stand and try by his testimony to criticise McClellan's movements, is, to say the least, very *unique*.

Leaving the correctness or incorrectness of the average march of six miles per day, as completely irrelevant, untested, we shall consider how General Halleck is justified in designating, as he does, an average march of six miles per day as censurably slow, by placing the word *only* before *six miles;* we will beforehand give him credit, however, for the new idea that there ever has existed, or does now exist, any regulation as to the rate of speed with which an army has to repel an invading enemy. Comparison with the movements of other armies under similar circumstances will best enable us to come to a proper conclusion on this point.

General Pope, if we are well informed, was put in command of the Army of Virginia and was ordered to *repel* the rebel forces crossing the Rappahannock: on the 14th day of July last, *he*, in his first order to the officers and soldiers of his army, says:

"I have spent two weeks in learning your whereabouts, your condition and your wants; in preparing you for active operations and in placing you in positions from which you can act promptly and to the purpose."

That dashing general, when ordered "*to repel an invading enemy,*" with an army in fine condition, two thirds of which had hardly lost a man in an engagement, required two weeks to put himself and his army in, what he considered, a proper position. Toward the enemy he had not advanced an inch.

General McClellan was put in command of that same army after it had been routed and demoralized, and far more than decimated, under Mr. Pope, on the 2d day of September. On the 4th he assumed command, and on the 17th day of September, after having won two others, he fought and won the great battle of Antietam; on the 19th he occupied the banks of the Potomac, had actually *repelled* the invading enemy, and had completed in two weeks, one of the most brilliant campaigns on record. Halleck, in his report of the Pope campaign, does not say a single word about the average rate of speed per day with which he moved in *pursuit* of the invader, nor with which he performed the reverse movement.

If our conceptions of military operations are not entirely wrong, it was General Halleck's object, and he was under orders, to *repel* the invading army under Beauregard after their attempt to drive Grant's corps of Halleck's army, into the Tennessee River at Pittsburgh Landing, April 5th, 1862. It took General Halleck until May 29th, that is fifty-five days, to, what he calls, *pursue* the invading enemy to Corinth, a distance of about twenty miles, or at a rate of speed of a little over *a third part of a mile per day*. At Corinth, for reasons publicly as yet unknown, he stopped *repelling* and *pursuing* altogether, allowed his generals to go a-travelling, his large army gradually to dwindle away, and permitted the enemy unmolested to reinforce the rebel army massed around Richmond against the Army of the Potomac.

Between May 7th and July 2nd, 1862, in fifty six days, McClellan, with the army of the Potomac, fought the battles of Williamsburg, West Point, Fair Oaks, Mechanicsville, Hanover Court-House, Savage Station, Gaine's Mill, White Oak Swamp, Cross-roads and Malvern Hill; and thereby secured for his name a place in history, on her scroll of fame, side by side with the few *great strategists* endowed with a military genius of the highest order. Never for a day would he leave his noble army, not even to see the President: Mr. Lincoln had to go to see the General in camp, at Harrison's Landing, as well as on the upper Potomac among the half-clad, bare-footed heroes of Antietam.

Such is McClellan, whose strategic movements on his march to save the Administration, had to be criticised before a commission; who had not asked the General to appear before them, and thereby showed that they considered his acts entirely unconnected with the Harper's Ferry affair, which they had to investigate; and such is William H. Halleck, *General-in-Chief of the army of the United States*, the witness upon whose *opinion* the censure of George B. McClellan is based because he pursues too slow.

We have investigated the report of the Harper's Ferry commissioners at some length, because this report convinced us that the intrigues in Washington were at work again, at work against McClellan, against the army, and consequently against the best interests of the country. It showed that the President's promises would not be fulfilled; it threw the first light on the origin of what we consider a most unpardonable strategical blunder; it showed us that the miserable plan for the Fall campaign can not be charged against General McClellan.

In the execution of this plan, the army of the Potomac had with brilliant success occupied all the mountain passes from Gregory Gap to Manassas Gap. Thoroughfare Gap and Warrenton were in our possession; *the headquarters of the commanding General were at Rectertown.* A snow storm swept over the mountains, when at midnight of Nov. 7, General Buckingham arrived at headquarters and handed to McClellan the following order:

GENERAL ORDERS—No. 182.
War Department, Adjutant-General's Office,
Washington, Nov. 5, 1862.

By direction of the President of the United States, it is ordered that Major-General McClellan be relieved from the command of the army of the Potomac, and that Major-General Burnside take the command of that army. By order of the Secretary of War.

E. M. Townsend, A. A. General.

McClellan at once surrendered his command to General Burnside, and issued the following address to his army:

> HEADQUARTERS ARMY OF THE POTOMAC,
> CAMP NEAR RECTORTOWN, VA.. Nov. 7, 1862.
>
> *Officers and Soldiers of the Army of the Potomac:*
> An order of the President devolves upon Major-General Burnside the command of this army. In parting from you I cannot express the love and gratitude I bear to you. As an army, you have grown up under my care. In you I have never found doubt or coldness. The battles you have fought under my command will proudly live in our nation's history. The glory you have achieved ; our mutual perils and fatigues ; the graves of our comrades'fallen in battle and by disease ; the broken forms of those wounds and sickness have disabled—the strongest associations which can exist among men, unite us still by an indissoluble tie. We shall ever be comrades in supporting the Constitution of our country and the nationality of its people.
>
> GEORGE B. McCLELLAN,
> Major-General U. S. A.

He then went with Burnside and all the staff officers to bid farewell to the several corps of the army, who were drawn up in line, and received him with military salutes. "Don't let him go!" "Bring him back!" "He must not go!" and similar were the exclamations of thousands upon thousands of our brave veteran soldiers, who under their General, and by his example had learned to stand cool and firm in the face of death, because their country's cause demanded it, and to be humane and courteous towards an unarmed enemy because their country's cause demanded that also.

We have seen letters of officers and private soldiers belonging to that army; they all express the grief, the sorrow, the deep dissatisfaction of the army over the removal of their beloved General.

On reaching the railway station to take the cars, a salute was fired ; the troops drawn up in line, afterwards broke ranks and many called for a few parting words. While on the platform of the railroad depot he said in response :

"Stand by Burnside as you have stood by me, and all will be well. Good bye."

When the news of General McClellan's removal from command was published, it was accompanied by the following letter from General Halleck to the Hon. E. M. Stanton, Secretary of War, and a telegraphic dispatch from General McClellan to General Meigs, Quarter-Master General :

HEADQUARTERS OF THE ARMY,
WASHINGTON, October 28, 1862.

Hon. E. M. STANTON, *Secretary of War.*

SIR:—In reply to the general interrogatories contained in your letter of yesterday, I have to report:

1. That requisitions for supplies to the army under General McClellan are made by his staff officers on the Chiefs of Bureaus here; that is, for Quartermaster's supplies, by his Chief Quartermaster on the Quarter-Master-General; for Commissary supplies, by his Chief Commissary on the Commissary-General, &c. No such requisitions have been, to my knowledge made upon the Secretary of War, and none upon the General-in-Chief.

2. On several occasions Gen. McClellan has telegraphed to me that his army was deficient in certain supplies. All these telegrams were immediately referred to the heads of Bureaus with orders to report. It was ascertained that in every instance the requisitions had been immediately filled, except one, where the Quartermaster-General had been obliged to send from Philadelphia certain articles of clothing, tents, &c., not having a full supply here. There has not been, so far as I could ascertain, any neglect or delay in any Department or Bureau, in issuing all supplies asked for by Gen. McClellan or by the officers of his staff. Delays have occasionally occurred in forwarding supplies by rail, on account of the crowded condition of the depots, or of a want of cars; but whenever notified of this, agents have been sent out to remove the difficulty. Under the excellent superintendence of General Haupt, I think these delays have been less frequent and of shorter duration than is usual with freight trains. An army of the size of that under General McClellan will frequently be for some days without the supplies asked, on account of neglect in making timely requisitions, and unavoidable delays in forwarding them, and in distributing them to the different brigades and regiments.

From all the information I can obtain, I am of opinion that the requisitions from that army have been filled more promptly, and that the men, as a general rule, have been better supplied, than our armies operating in the West. The latter have operated at much greater distances from the the sources of supply, and have had far less facilities for transportation. In fine, I believe no armies in the world, while in campaign, have been more promptly or better supplied than ours.

3. Soon after the battle of Antietam, Gen. McClellan was urged to give me information of his intended movements, in order that if he moved between the enemy and Washington, reinforcements could be sent from this place. On the first of October, finding that he purposed to operate from Harper's Ferry, I urged him to cross the river at once and give battle to the enemy, pointing out to him the disadvantages of delaying till the Autumn rains had swollen the Potomac and impaired the roads. On the 6th of October he was peremptorily ordered to "cross the Potomac and give battle to the enemy or drive him South. Your army *must* move now while the roads are good." It will be observed that three weeks have passed since this order was given.

4. In my opinion there has been no such want of supplies in the army under General McClellan as to prevent his compliance with the orders to advance against the enemy. Had he moved to the South side of the Potomac, he could have received his supplies almost as regularly as by remaining inactive on the north.

On the 7th of October, in a telegram in regard to his intended movements, Gen. McClellan stated that it would require at least three days to supply the First, Fifth and Sixth Corps, that they needed shoes and other indispensable articles of clothing, as well as shelter tents. No complaint was made that any requisitions had not been filled, and it was inferred from his language that he was only waiting for the distribution of his supplies. On the 11th he telegraphed that a portion of his supplies sent by rail had been delayed.

As already stated, agents were immediately sent from here to investigate this complaint, and they reported that everything had gone forward. On the same day (the 11th) he spoke of many of his horses being broken down by fatigue. On the 12th he complained that the rate of supply was only "150 horses per week for the entire army there and in front of Washington." I immediately directed the Quartermaster-General to inquire into this matter, and report why a larger supply was not furnished. Gen. Meigs reported on the 14th that the average issue of horses to Gen. McClellan's army in the field and in front of Washington for the previous six weeks, had been 1,450 per week, or 8,754 in all. In addition, that large number of mules had been supplied, and that the number of animals with General McClellan's army on the Upper Potomac was over thirty-one thousand. He also reported that he was then sending to that army all the horses he could procure.

On the 18th, Gen. McClellan stated, in regard to Gen. Meigs' report that he had filled every requisition for shoes and clothing, "Gen. Meigs may have ordered these articles to be forwarded, but they have not reached our depots; and unless greater effort to insure prompt transmission is made by the department of which Gen. Meigs is the head, they might as well remain in New York or Philadelphia, so for as this army is concerned." I immediately called General Meigs' attention to this apparent neglect of his department. On the 25th he reported as the result of his investigation that 48,000 pairs of boots and shoes had been received by the Quartermaster of Gen. McClellan's army at Harper's Ferry, Frederick, and Hagerstown; that 20,000 pairs were at Harper's Ferry depot on the 21st; that 10,000 more were on their way, and 15,000 more ordered. Col. Ingals, Aid-de-Camp, and Chief Quartermaster to Gen. McClellan, telegraphed on the 25th, "The suffering for want of clothing is exaggerated, I think, and certainly might have been avoided by timely requisitions of regimental and brigade commanders." On the 26th he telegraphed to the Quartermaster-General that the clothing was not detained in cars at the depots. "Such complaints are groundless. The fact is, the clothing arrives and is issued, but more is still wanted. I have ordered more than would seem necessary from any data furnished me, and I beg to remind you that you have always very promptly met my requisitions so far as clothing is concerned. Our depot is not at fault. It provides as soon as due notice is given. I foresee no time when an army of over 100,000 men will not call for clothing and other articles."

In regard to General McClellan's means of promptly communicating the wants of his army to me or to the proper Bureaus of the War Department, I report that, in addition to the ordinary mails, he has been in hourly communication with Washington by telegraph.

It is due to Gen. Meigs that I should submit herewith a copy of a telegram received by him from Gen. McClellan.

Very respectfully your obedient servant,

H. W. HALLECK, General-in-Chief.

UNITED STATES MILITARY TELEGRAPH.

[Received Oct. 22, 1862—9:40 P. M.]

From McClellan's Headquarters.

To Brigadier-General Meigs:—Your dispatch of this date is received. I have never intended, in any letter or dispatch, to make any accusation against yourself or your Department for not furnishing or forwarding clothing as rapidly as it was possible for you to do. I believe that everything has been done that could be done in this respect. The idea that I have tried to convey was, that certain portions of the command were without clothing, and the army could not move until it was supplied.

G. B. McCLELLAN, M. G.

The removal of the commanding General of a large army, moving against a not distant enemy, is an event, of necessity pregnant with grave consequences for good or for evil, to the power ordering the removal, to the country, and to the General deprived of command. This threefold importance demands a minute investigation and scrutiny of everything conducive to the development of the motives and reasons for so consequential proceedings. The publication of the two documents referred to, simultaneously with the news of the removal of McClellan, point them out as explaining the culminating cause, that *justifies* the all important step.

General Halleck's letter of October 28 is written in reply to general interrogatories presented by Mr. Stanton on the *day previous.* Its extent, its completeness, the numerous facts contained therein, requiring references to books, and an extensive correspondence, the unusual importance of the object for which, undoubtedly, it is intended, demanding great care and deliberation in its preparation—all this proves either, that General Halleck is a man of astonishing business qualification, who has all the minutiæ of his extensive official transactions at his finger's ends, and who possesses an enviable and unerring memory for executive details; or that the document had been carefully prepared, anterior to its date, to serve an important end in view. For the better understanding of the document in question, we give Mr. Edwin M. Stanton's letter containing the several interrogatories to which General Halleck's forms the reply:

EXHIBIT NO. 5.

War Department, Washington City, Oct. 27, 1862.

General: It has been publicly stated that the army under General McClellan has been unable to move during the fine weather of this fall, for want of shoes, clothing and other supplies. You will please report to this Department upon the following points:

1. To whom and in what manner the requisitions for supplies to the army under General McClellan have been made since you assumed com-

mand as General-in-Chief, and whether any requisition for supplies of any kind has since that time been made upon the Secretary of War, or communication had with him, except through you.

2. If you, as General-in-Chief, have taken pains to ascertain the condition of the army in respect to supplies of shoes, clothing, arms, and other necessaries, and whether there has been any neglect or delay by any Department or Bureau, in filling the requisitions for supplies; and what has been and is the condition of that army, as compared with other armies in respect to supplies.

3. At what time after the battle of Antietam the orders to advance against the enemy were given to General McClellan, and how often have they been repeated.

4. Whether, in your opinion, there has been any want in the army, under General McClellan, of shoes, clothing, arms, or other equipments or supplies, that ought to have prevented its advance against the enemy, when the order was given.

5. How long was it after the orders to advance were given to General McClellan, before he informed you that any shoes or clothing were wanted in his army, and what are his means of communicating the wants of the army to you, or the proper bureau of the War Department.

Yours truly,   EDWIN M. STANTON,
Secretary of War.

Major-General HALLECK, General-in-Chief.
OFFICIAL.

This letter to the General-in-Chief, for transparent reasons, was not given to the public when the reply thereto was ordered to be published: its later appearance in the Report of General Halleck, to the author of the letter, completes a chain of evidence which would have been imperfect without it.

We see the Secretary of War and the General-in-Chief of the army of the United States enter into a correspondence with each other for the purpose of asking questions and eliciting answers on matters about which the questioner ought to be by far better informed than the respondent; evidently with the intention to convince the people that General McClellan, or some one on his behalf, has without actual cause, complained of want in the army of the Potomac of shoes, clothing and other supplies; and that this imaginary want has been used as a pretext why the army was not led into Virginia; that General McClellan in not moving the army across the Potomac has become guilty of disobedience to orders, and that consequently the Administration had to deprive him of his command.

As to the first part, we have already stated that the want existed, and we have enumerated some of the causes by which it had been produced.* Let us see how the two high correspondents succeeded

---

* General Pope's orders to General Banks, and General Porter's report to General Burnside, produced in Porter's court martial, fully confirms our statements.

in disproving by the pen what a hundred thousand soldiers by their pains and sufferings knew to be the truth.

To Mr. Stanton's first question, the Secretary of War is the most competent person to give a satisfactory answer. To designate the persons to whom, and regulate the manner in which, requisitions for supplies are to be made by the commanders of all armies; to see that they are properly made and punctually supplied, is one of the most important duties of that functionary. The Secretary of War is in all countries considered, and frequently called the mother of the army, and the commander-in-chief the father; the mother has to procure, prepare and serve out her supplies, that with the well clad, well fed, and well armed boys the father may protect against the enemy, the common fireside, our country. The part Mr. Stanton has undertaken to act as commander-in-chief over the corps under Gens. McDowell, Banks and Fremont had brought disgrace and ruin over the country, and had filled tens of thousands of new dug graves while it lasted; but it can never relieve the honorable Secretary of his duties, after he had so miscarried as a commander that even Mr. Lincoln could not endure it any longer, and had to stop him in his mad career. The chief Quartermaster, the chief Commissary, the chief of Ordnance, and all the other chiefs of Bureaus, are the subordinates, and perform every official act in behalf, and under the instructions of the Secretary of War, and in his name they report to him, who is just as much accountable for all their performances as the commanding general of an army is accountable for the official acts of any of his staff officers, which are all performed in his name and on his behalf, and reported to him.

For the very purpose that the Secretary of War should be entirely relieved from all connection with and care of the strategical and purely military affairs of the army, General Halleck was appointed General-in-Chief; and the supervision and general direction of the strategical and military affairs vested in him. If, as Mr. Stanton tries to make us believe, the care for supplies, etc, had also been put upon General Halleck's shoulders, then it is clear that the latter would have to perform all the duties heretofore exercised by our Secretary of war, and that Mr. Stanton would occupy a perfect sinecure. The sentence attached to this first question is intended to shield the honorable Secretary from the consequences, which on account of his previous unpardonable interference with the purely military affairs of the army, the future may yet have in store for him. He desires to prove that of late he has not interfered. The answer of General Halleck to this question shows that the communications of General McClellan with the Secretary of War have been carried on as they ought to be, through their respective representative quarter-masters' commissaries. It also states that no requisitions have been made upon him.

Mr. Stanton's second question is in its first sentence, rather perplexing for General Halleck :—" Have you *as Commander-in-Chief* TAKEN PAINS to ascertain the condition of the army in regard to certain supplies ?" The General not being able to answer this delicate but direct question in the affirmative, does not answer it at all; of which neglect the Secretary, for the present, does not seem to take any further notice, and slides immediately to the second section of his question; to which he answers that on *several* occasions McClellan has telegraphed to him that his army was deficient in certain supplies, and that he (Halleck) had referred *all* these telegrams immediately to the heads of Bureaus, *to report*—not to supply. Also that it was ascertained that in one instance the requisition for certain articles of clothing, tents *et cetera*, (which may mean, some very important things) had to be got from Philadelphia ; that *occasionally* delays in forwarding supplies by rail had occurred, but that whenever *notified* of this—(by whom ?)—*agents have been sent out* to remove the difficulty—(on the railroad ?)—that delays have been less frequent, and of shorter duration than is *usual* with *freight trains*. Freight trains usually are slow but not sure ; supplies for the army ought to be rapid and sure : this sentence shows how incompetent are the heads and hands upon whom our soldiers rely for their necessaries.*
That the armies in the West have been supplied less promptly than the army under McClellan may be correct, as far as the operations of those armies led them away from the navigable rivers; but we believe, in favor of General Halleck, that the slow and imperfect supplies of his army of the West, contributed to the fact that it took him as we have shown above, fifty-two days to move twenty miles, while McClellan's army in the same number of days fought ten battles, and marched several hundred miles; and at another time commenced and completed a brilliant campaign in a fortnight.

---

* All of this shows that the PAINS the *Commander-in-Chief* has taken to ascertain the condition of the army, have been taken at a great distance from the army, in his comfortable office at Washington, and consisted in receiving many requests, which he referred to the heads of bureaus ; but *that he did not go near that army.*

Mr. Stanton's third question is again of the character that the honorable Secretary ought to have answered it as well as anybody in the world, because in the telegram of October 6, annexed to General Halleck's report of Dec. 2d, which he erroneously called a *peremptory Order*, the General distinctly says : " I am directed to add that the *Secretary of War* and the *General-in-Chief* fully concur with the President in these *instructions*. The honorable Secretary, therefore, must have had a copy of the telegram on file.

Mr. Stanton's fifth and last question is a leading one. He wishes to have it understood that McClellan did not complain of want of shoes or clothing *until after he was ordered to advance*. General Halleck, in answer 5, meets the honorable Secretary half way by referring at once to October 7, a day or two after the so-called peremptory order ; but he has, in the lengthy answer No. 2, enumerated a long list of well-founded complaints made by McClellan, *all* previous to the 6th of October, and *all* of which the General-in-Chief has explained to *his own* satisfaction.

In his 6th reply General Halleck states in substance that McClellan telegraphed to him on Oct. 11 that his supplies by rail had been delayed, and that many of his horses had been broken down ; Oct. 12th that he was supplied only at the *rate* of 150 horses per week. The first complaint brought the *Agents*, (Sec. 2,) on the road, *but the delay existed and had to be endured* by the army. The second complaint, caused undoubtedly by the enormous fatigue which the cavalry had to undergo in following General Stuart's horses in their raid in Pennsylvania and Maryland, which took place *two days before the* 12*th*, seems to have been entirely misunderstood by General Meigs, who represents to Halleck how many *mules* and *animals* are attached to the army, and gives an *average* furnished during 6 *weeks;* which brings it back into August, when Pope had not yet distinguished himself.

On the 18th of October, about *thirty days* after the battle of Antietam, McClellan says in substance, the supplies which General Meigs says he has sent have *not reached our depot*, and they might as well remain *in New York* or Philadelphia, so far as this army was concerned. Meigs, who is ordered on the 18th to report *immediately*, and who, in his brilliant offices in Washington, undisturbed by war ; from his way bills, and the return of his wagon guards and conductors under command of General Haupt, ought to be able to tell *within a few hours* when and what he has sent to the army, and if, when and where it has been delivered and receipted for, takes till the 25th

—as long time as it took McClellan to fight the seven battles on the peninsula ; half as long as the entire Maryland campaign—long after McClellan's army had entered Virginia, to make a report, that on the 21st, *three days after McClellan's complaint reached Washington,* 48,000 pair of boots and shoes had been delivered to the Quartermaster of McClellan's army, that 20,000 pair were lying at the Harper's Ferry Depot, not *with McClellan's army;* that 10,000 pair were on their way—*he does not know where;* and 15,000 pair were ordered—*he does not say where and when.*

As General Meigs, with the telegraph facilities referred to by General Halleck at his disposal, does not report that any shoes or boots had actually reached any depot of McClellan's army on or before October 18th, it is safe to say that according to General Halleck's and General Meigs's own statement, McClellan's army was four weeks after the battle of Antietam without proper shoes and boots—and that on the 25th of October, about *half as many* pair of shoes and boots as the army required had been delivered—and that when all the shoes and boots which General Meigs reports as on their way and as ordered, without any fixed time for delivery, (amounting to about 90,000 pairs,) should one of these days reach the army of over 100,000 men, that then some 10,000 of our brave soldiers will yet have to go barefooted.

On the 25th of October, a week after McClellan's complaint of the 18th, Colonel Ingal's Quartermaster-General to General McClellan telegraphs, " *The suffering for want of clothing is exaggerated.*"

This officer of the Quartermaster (that is of the War Department) has no further consolation for the Secretary of War and for Mr. Halleck than to say, the *suffering* for the want of clothing is exaggerated : not the want—the want he admits; he officially states that the want has been so great that it has caused *suffering;* that the suffering still exists, but that on the 25th day of October, *two days* before, the Honorable Secretary, whose office is next door to that of the General-in-Chief, writes the interrogation to the latter, the *suffering* is exaggerated—relieved but not removed. But how was it five weeks before the 25th day of October, immediately after Antietam, when that cry of suffering first startled the country, and before, during thirty-five long days, urged by McClellan's again and again repeated demands, the Secretary of War, through the Chief Quartermaster, had gradually relieved some of the suffering, half-naked army ?

Colonel Ingal's remarks, "*that he foresees no time when an army of over 100,000 men will not call for clothing or other articles*" is correct. It expresses the experience made by all the armies in the world. But if this fact is known it should have the result it produces in other armies: it should beget the fostering care, which, under the guidance of the Secretary of War, through his subordinates, causes a *constant expedition* of supplies to reach the army regularly at certain short intervals without extra requisition; which, in other armies, makes the mother of the army, (who stays at home, and who has time to order, to examine, and to dispatch the necessary food, clothing, arms and ammunition,) the need of which she knows just as well as the General can tell her, makes the Secretary of War attend to all these matters, and thereby relieve the Commanding General and his Staff, who have always as much to attend to as they possibly can stand, from the additional care of asking and enumerating things which everybody knows the army regularly wants.

General McClellan's telegram, October 22d, to Quartermaster-General Meigs, confirms, the assertion of all the subordinates of the Secretary of War, that each of them has done all they possibly could do to supply the army of the Potomac, to the contrary, notwithstanding, *that certain portions of the army were then without clothing, and that the army could not move till it was supplied.*

We believe we have proved, from the official statement of the General-in-Chief himself, that the army of the Potomac has suffered from and was unable to move on account of want of shoes, clothing, and other supplies. We have declared that according to well established rules, it is in all countries the duty of the War Department to furnish supplies, and to regulate and supervise their transportation to the army, which, of course, cannot have any benefit of them till they have been delivered; and that the Secretary of War, under whose orders all the different chiefs of bureaus are acting, is the officer responsible for any want of the most systematic, effective and perfect regulation, and execution in all matters connected with the subsistence and supplies of the army.

To attain the means of introducing system and punctuality in the transportation of supplies to our armies, the Secretary of War took, at an early day, possession of all the railroads connecting the several armies with the central depot—Washington—and established a bureau of construction and operation of United States Military railroads. To the Chief of this bureau the Secretary appointed General H. Haupt, who has his office at the War Department, immediately under the eyes of the honorable Secretary; and acts, of course, under the general directions, and on behalf of that high officer. As the representative of the Secretary of War, he exercises *supreme* control over the railroads.

That there had been frequent and long delays in the transportation of the supplies, from the want of which the army under General McClellan was suffering; that those delays were caused by the unsystematic, irregular, and ineffective management of this branch of the Department; that these delays occurred and continued to take place from the moment the army of the Potomac entered Maryland, till after it had marched to Virginia; that these delays, as well as the fact that they were caused by an imperfect and unsystematic, and therefore improper, management of the military railroads under the War Department, were well known to the Secretary of War and to the General-in-Chief of the army of the United States; that consequently that part of the correspondence between the two last named high personages, 27th and 28th October, 1862, referring to the suffering of McClellan's army, to its causes, and to the time when it existed, has been carried on under false pretences, for the purpose of hiding their own neglect or incompetence from the public eye, and manufacturing false evidence against General McClellan:—All this is proved by the order of General Haupt, to whom General Halleck refers in his letter October 28, to Mr. Stanton, addressed to the post, quartermasters, commissaries, officers and agents of military railroads, dated†

WAR DEPARTMENT, U. S. MILITARY RAIL ROADS, }
WASHINGTON, Nov. 10, 1862. }

To Post Quartermasters, Commissaries, Officers and Agents of Military Railroads:

GENTLEMEN: The exceedingly critical condition of affairs compels me to address you this circular, and to endeavor, with all the earnestness and force of language I can command, to explain some of the difficulties connected with military railroad transportation, and ask your co-operation and assistance in forwarding supplies.

The army is dependent for its supplies upon a single-track railroad, in bad condition, without sidings of sufficient length, without wood, with a short supply of water, and with insufficient equipments. This road is taxed with an amount of business equal to the ordinary freights of a large city—an amount four times as large as it has ever before been called upon to accommodate, and twice as large as I reported to Gen. McClellan its capacity for transportation.

---

†The fact that General Haupt in behalf of the Secretary of War, did not discover the remedy for the existing irregularities, and long and frequent delays—and did not instruct his subordinates how to obviate and overcome them till two days after General McClellan had transferred his command, so that the army could not derive any benefit from the improved management of this branch of the War Department, while he commanded it—all of this speaks for itself. The necessity of the numerous and important improvements introduced by this order proves the wretched condition the transportation service must have been in before.

There cannot be the most distant prospect of keeping the army supplied without constant uninterrupted movement of trains day and night. The delicate machinery of the road must not be deranged by any detention or interference; it must be directed by one mind, and one only. No one, not even myself, must derange the plans of the superintendent, vary his instructions, or direct his subordinates. Cars must be loaded and unloaded with the utmost expedition possible, and kept in motion. Convenience must not be consulted; unload the cars anywhere, and move their contents afterwards, or issue where they lie; do not delay or require cars to be shifted, or trains moved, simply to avoid inconvenience. Railroad employees must be civil; they must do anything in their power to accommodate officers if it will not delay trains, but if it will cause delay, their orders are peremptory; they must decline, Do not quarrel with them, or refuse to unload cars because they are not in the most convenient positions; in doing this you not only prevent the forwarding of supplies, but derange movements dependent upon the prompt return of cars. If employees are uncivil or unaccommodating, report the facts to me. * *

* * Again I say that if the army is to be supplied, the condition which, in its importance transcends all others, is that no delay, not even a minute, should be allowed to occur in unloading cars, if it can be avoided. Movement, unceasing movement in the trains, is our only salvation; without it the army must retreat or starve. Would that I could express its importance as I felt it. * * * * The Secretary of War and the commanding General of the army fully understand and appreciate the fact, that the operations of a railroad must be directed by one mind, even if it should not be a superior one. They have declared that my control over the railroads is "*supreme*," and that "no military officer has any authority to interfere with it." But I do not wish to exercise "authority." I prefer to appeal to the patriotism and good sense of those whose business brings them in contact with the railway managers, and believe that the appeal will not be in vain, when I ask their assistance and co-operation. * * * * I hope that I have made myself understood, and that officers of all grades will receive these explanations in the spirit in which they are given.

Agents on United States military railroads, at each depot station, are required to report daily to the superintendent, as follows:

1. The exact time of arrival of each train, and the numbers of the cars which it contains,
2. The force employed to unload it.
3. If there was a sufficient force to unload each and every car at the same time.
4. The time actually occupied in unloading.
5. The name of the officer or officers who superintended the unloading.
6. All cases of detention to cars, engines or trains, and their causes.

The time occupied in unloading cars should be employed by the engineer and conductor, whenever practicable, in procuring wood and water, and in doing whatever else may be necessary to permit an immediate return.

          H. HAUPT, Brigadier-General,
In charge of construction and operation of United States Military Railroads,

In section three of the letter of October 28th, General Halleck tries to produce the impression that McClellan had been guilty of disobedience to his orders. If he does not succeed, it is not for want of artful phraseology.

If, as he desires to make it appear, General Halleck had any right whatever to give orders to General McClellan, after what had taken place between the defeat of Mr. Pope, and the preservation of the administration by McClellan, from captivity by General Lee—if he was General-in-Chief over McClellan—it was *his* duty to *make* the general plan of the new campaign, and order McClellan to carry it out. In that case he did neither understand nor do his duty when he asked McClellan *for information of his intended movements.* He would not have been in a position of *finding that he purposed to operate from Harper's Ferry, and to urge him to cross the river at once*, but he would have fixed the place whence, and at what time the operations were to be commenced, and would have ordered the execution thereof. He would in that case have been able to say in his closing sentence, "*I ordered him peremptorily to cross,*" and he would have been bound, in duty to the army, in duty to his country and in duty to his high office as General in Chief, to have General McClellan at once put under arrest, and tried before a court martial on the grave charge "*of disobedience of orders to attack the enemy,*" the punishment of which is one of the most severe. Knowing, of course, that the immediate attack was necessary for the welfare of the army and of the country—knowing the dangers that might follow even a short delay in the execution of this movement, by his keeping silent for over three weeks,‡—and by not taking official action in this matter of highest importance until he had received a general interrogatory from the honorable Secretary of War; (which silence costs the country tens of millions) General Halleck, in our opinion, has himself become guilty of willful neglect of duty, for which in every other army in the civilized world, he would be court martialed. He is even not entitled to the palliation of his offence, on the plea of friendly sentiments towards a distinguished brother officer, highest in rank in the army, who has always deserved well of his country; because throughout these entire transactions we have been unable to discover any but the most unfriendly and unsoldierly sentiments on behalf of the General-in-Chief towards General McClellan.

‡ It is well known that on the 28th day of October, when General Halleck made that statement, the army of the Potomac had crossed according to Halleck's report to the Secretary of War, October 26, and was at Upperville and Snickersville in the Blue Ridge.

The telegraphic dispatch of Oct. 6th, 1862, from General Halleck to McClellan reads :

"I am instructed to telegraph you as follows: The *President directs* that you cross * * * * It is necessary that the plan of your operations be positively determined upon before orders are given for building bridges and repairing railroads. * * * * I am directed to add that the Secretary of War and the General-in-Chief fully concur with the President in these instructions.

"H. W. HALLECK, General-in-Chief."

General Halleck, in his Report to the Secretary of War, Dec. 2d., 1862, of McClellan says :

"What caused him to change his views, or what his plan of campaign was, I am ignorant, for about this time he ceased to communicate with me in regard to his operations, sending his reports direct to the President. On the 5th ultimo I received the written order of the President relieving General McClellan, and placing General Burnside in command of the Army of the Potomac."

In his examination by the Commission to investigate the disastrous battle of Fredericksburg, General Halleck, *under oath*, testified, that all the troops in Washington were "under command of General McClellan, that he gave his orders direct to the commanding officers at Washington, with one single exception that no troops should be moved from the command at Washington until I was notified by General McClellan or the commanding officer here (Washington)." Which statement means, that besides the troops in Virginia and Maryland, those in and around Washington were also under direct command of General McClellan. "General Burnside, I was told, held the same position when he relieved him." (The General made this statement to show that he could not be held responsible for any action or omission in the matter under investigation.)

In September last, when General McClellan left Washington for the Maryland campaign, he entrusted the command of the forces in the fortifications around that city to General Banks; the latter issued an order to his army stating, that by order of Major-General McClellan he assumed command, &c.

From all these facts, and from the statements in section 3 of General Halleck's letter of October 28th, we come to the conclusion that on the 1st of September last when President Lincoln, forced by absolute necessity, requested General McClellan to resume command, the latter, as a condition *sine qua non*, demanded that henceforward no person whatever, but in particular not the Secretary of War or the General-in-Chief, should have any right to interfere with, or to give orders, or to control him and the armies under his command, or their operations, and that all necessary deliberations, consultations and communications regarding his armies and their movements, should be direct from the President to the General and *vice versa*, and that to the President of the United States alone he would be accountable. The President accepted this condition, and pledged himself strictly to adhere to it; the Secretary of War and the General-in-Chief had to and did submit to it.

The brilliant campaign in Maryland would have been impossible had any one interfered with McClellan.

As neither the Secretary of War nor the General-in-Chief had, per special agreement, any right to give orders or instructions to General McClellan, it is clear that, as these two officers failed to disprove the suffering of the army from want of shoes, clothing, &c., so they have failed to prove their insinuation that General McClellan had been guilty of disobedience to their orders.

The imminent personal danger removed from the portals of the White House and the War Department, the Secretary of War and the General-in-Chief began to feel uneasy and uncomfortable under the agreement in question, and the President grew less exact in the fulfillment of his promise.

The General-in-Chief was curious to know McClellan's plan for the next campaign, and was not let into the secret because McClellan and the country had almost been ruined when in March last, yielding to official pressure, he explained his plan, whereupon it became immediately known to the rebel General Johnson.*

The General-in-Chief thereupon *urged* McClellan to decide between two plans—either of them bad, but they alone appear within the range of General Halleck's strategical mind. General McClellan did not enter into any correspondence with him, and his curiosity was not satisfied.

On the 6th of October the General-in-Chief caused himself to be *instructed* by the President to telegraph to General McClellan a most remarkable dispatch.

WASHINGTON, D. C., October 6, 1862.

MAJOR-GENERAL McCLELLAN: I am instructed to telegraph you as follows: The President directs that you cross the Potomac and give battle to the enemy or drive him South. Your army must move now while the roads are good. If you cross the river between the enemy and Washington, and cover the latter by your operation, you can be reinforced with 30,000 men. If you move up the valley of the Shenandoah, not more

---

* "Army of the Potomac." By Prince Joinville.

than 12,000 or 15,000 can be sent to you. The President advises the interior line between Washington and the enemy, but does not order it. He is very desirous that your army move as soon as possible. You will immediately report what line you adopt and when you intend to cross the river. Also to what point the reinforcements are to be sent. It is necessary that the plan of your operations be positively determined on before orders are given for building bridges and repairing railroads. I am directed to add that the Secretary of War and the General-in-Chief fully concur with the President in these instructions.

H. W. HALLECK, General-in-Chief.

" *The President directs that you cross the Potomac and give battle to the enemy or drive him South ; your army must now move while the roads are good.*" This reads almost as if a definite plan of the campaign had been decided upon by the President, and that the execution thereof had been ordered ; but the balance of the dispatch contains numerous questions, suggestions and propositions, all intended to draw from McClellan a disclosure of his actual plan for the campaign, and all referring exclusively to the two plans previously alluded to by the General-in-Chief, of which the President orders General Halleck to say, " that he *advises* but does not *order* it." (This latter would have been contrary to agreement with General McClellan.) " *It is necessary that the plan of your operations be positively determined upon before orders are given for building bridges and repairing railroads*" shows the endeavor to learn McClellan's plan, as well as that the latter had requested *bridges* and *railroads* to be repaired ; a point, the importance of which we shall hereafter take occasion to explain.

" *I am directed to add that the Secretary of War and the General-in-Chief fully concur with the President in these instructions.*" This closing sentence shows that the President submits his opinion in the matter first to Mr. Stanton and General Halleck, and asked for their concurrence ; this secured he directs General Halleck to communicate these views to General McClellan, and to tell him that the President has asked Mr. Stanton's and Mr. Halleck's views, and that the Secretary of War and the General-in-Chief fully concur with the President.

This roundabout way to secure to the Commander of the army of the Potomac the benefit of the opinion of the Secretary of War and the General-in-Chief on the President's *strategical suggestions*, proves conclusively, we think, that both these high officials, by special agreement, were not permitted to communicate their views officially and direct to General McClellan.

To call the contradictory suggestions and the suggestive contradictions, forming the substance of this dispatch *instructions*, as the General-in-Chief does call them, is certainly a bold stretch of imagination —imagination is the most dangerous virtue in a general—but even this he exceeds when he refers to this telegram as a *peremptory order.* This dispatch constituted so direct a violation of stipulations made by General McClellan, that from that time the General ceased to have any further communication with either of the two concurring personages.

The documentary evidence from which we have drawn all the conclusions heretofore arrived at, it will be observed has all been "*ex parte,*" all of it having been furnished to us exclusively by Edwin M. Stanton, Secretary of War, and H. W. Halleck, General-in-Chief of the armies of the United States, who, on the 27th and 2t8h day of October last, entered into an exchange of notes for the purpose of demonstrating to the people that there existed good cause for the removal, on the 5th day of November, of Major-General McClellan from the command of the army of the Potomac. In this they have completely failed, and they have, by their own written statements, proved the utter mismanagement of the War Department and the ruinous consequences therefrom to the army and to the country.

Who can tell how much more disgusting and criminal their conduct will appear one of these days, when the self-sacrificing, patriotic general, whose true greatness made him the object of the hatred, the jealousy and the intrigues of those unprincipled men, may condescend to open his lips and permit publicity to be given to the damning evidence against them which he undoubtedly holds in his possession?

The President, after this, was more and more pressing in his demand that General McClellan should cross the Potomac, and McClellan was forced to choose between two evils: either to resign his command, which would have been inconsistent with good discipline and would have set a bad example; or, after having tried with all the arguments at his control to dissuade the President from the execution of, under existing circumstances, so unstrategical a movement, to act as he did in March, 1862—to perform his duty in the best possible manner.

The sentence in General Halleck's dispatch at the order of the President, October 6, "*it is necessary that the plan of your operations be fully determined upon before orders are given for building bridges and repairing railroads,*" seems to us to show that while McClellan still hoped to succeed in dissuading the President from the fatal plan to cross the Potomac at once, he was making all necessary preliminary preparations for the execution of the only sound strategy, the moment the President should have assented thereto. He wanted railroads repaired to move his army rapidly to the place of embarkation, say Alexandria, and bridges built for the same purpose; still he would not disclose his plan so that the enemy should know it. After full consideration of all the facts before us, we have no doubt that whenever General McClellan shall one of these days think it proper to permit his own plan for the fall campaign of 1862 to be published, it will, in all its principal points, coincide with the plan described in detail by us, and for which we have given reasons which, in our opinion, cannot well be disputed.

When the army of the Potomac had crossed the river near Berlin, General McClellan made his reports direct to the President; this of course vexed the Secretary of War and the General-in-Chief continually. Their influence over the President increased in equal ratio with the distance from Washington to the headquarters of the army of the Potomac; it was supreme on the 5th of November, when General Halleck succeeded in *receiving* the *written* order of the President relieving General McClellan and placing General Burnside in command of the army of the Potomac.

The Emperor of Russia, the most despotic military monarch in the world, would not deprive of command the highest officer in his army, who only two months before, at the head of 150,000 men, had saved his Government from destruction by an invading army, without having made known to the army the guilt of the General against whom he had taken so important a step.

The President of the United States has, on the 5th day of November, deprived of command Major-General McClellan, the highest ranked officer in the United States army, who in September had saved him and his Administration from the rebel General Lee.

On the first day of December the President sent a very long message to the representatives of the people, wherein want of space for a word of acknowledgment for their heroic devotion to the country's cause, to the army of half a million of citizen soldiers, compels him to refer the representatives, in all matters concerning the army, to the annual Report of the Secretary of War, the business of whose department exclusively comprises the army. The honorable Secretary's report, although rather brief, contains some valuable suggestions on the cultivation of Sea Island cotton, and on the question whether a liberated African is likely to establish his domicile North or South.

In matters concerning our Eastern armies the Secretary abstains from reporting, what, he says, the President knows as well as he does; on the removal of General McClellan he keeps a profound silence, and refers the President for all other matters, to the report made to him, the Secretary of War, by the General-in-Chief.

The General-in-Chief's Report to the Secretary of War is full. It contains details of great variety and interest; it refers to the correspondence between him and the Secretary of War, and in some respects it is explanatory thereto; but the General who, as we have seen, is not reluctant to report to the Secretary of War matters which the latter must know better than the General himself, does not even hint at what General McClellan has been guilty of, to deserve to be deprived of his command in the face of the enemy, a measure which the General well knew caused great dissatisfaction in the army as well as among the people at large.

The Secretary of War as well as the General-in-Chief, as we have seen, are both hostile to General McClellan, and have gone far out of their way for the purpose of injuring that General. The President's acts prove clearly that his sentiments toward General McClellan were congenial with those of Mr. Stanton and Mr. Halleck. No person can have the least doubt that, had it been in the power of the President, the Secretary of War, or the Commander-in-Chief, to assign even a half plausable excuse for the great wrong they had done to the General and to the army of the Potomac, they would willingly have published it.

The army has a right to know the reason why this removal took place. The silence on the subject in the Message, and in both the Reports, is most conclusive evidence that the Commander-in-Chief did not duly consider the welfare of the army in this unjustifiable military measure.

What an undisputable testimony as to the far-seeing intelligence, professional excellence and patriotism of General McClellan. What a triumph of the rectitude of his conduct, under the most provoking treatment and bad faith, on behalf of those whom naturally he had to consider his coöperaters and most reliable supporters in the energetic and successful conduct of the war. The Commander-in-Chief, the Secretary of War and the General-in-Chief, however eager they are to do so, neither by fair nor by foul means, can fasten a single censurable act or word upon General McClellan.

Notwithstanding the silence with which the General-in-Chief passes the reasons for the removal of General McClellan, his Report to the

Secretary of War, nevertheless, throws a flood of light on the operations of the army during the past year. In connection with some others, incidentally made public, it is the first document which officially sets at rest all doubts as to the men and measures that have prevented the operations of the army to result in the overthrow of the rebellion, and in the termination of this unholy war. To review the operations in the order in which they actually follow each other, we have to lay aside General Halleck's report, to return to it very soon.

Major-General McDowell had demanded a Court of Enquiry as to his conduct after the first battle of Bull Run. During the progress of these investigations there was presented in evidence elicited in the cross-examination—

1st. A letter of instructions by Major-General McClellan to the military Governor of the District of Columbia, Brigadier-General James S. Wadsworth, dated March 16, 1862.

2nd. A letter of instructions by Major-General McClellan to Major General Banks, commanding fifth corps, army of the Potomac, dated March 16, 1862.

These two documents give a most complete description of the dispositions made, and the means provided by the commander of the army of the Potomac, for the protection, and if need be, for the defence of the national capital, with its distant surroundings. They are master-pieces of clearness, of completeness, and of precision in strategical explanations and military orders, and they show that over 70,000 men, of all arms, had been put in and around the fortifications and strongly entrenched at Manassas and other principal points along the various lines of approach, to keep in check and repulse any force which might venture across the Rappahannock. So plain is the designation of the various strategical points selected, so precise the number of men, and the proportion in which they shall be composed of the various armies, that there exists no possibility for any person in sound mind, with only half a military idea, to misunderstand them or doubt their efficiency.

On the 1st day of April, 1862, when General McClellan embarked for the Peninsula, he sent to Brigadier-General L. Thomas, Adjutant-General U. S. Army, with the President and the Secretary of War, for the purpose of laying the same before the Secretary of War, a full and complete explanation of the disposition he had made, and of the number of troops designated for every commander, and to what place.*

---

* HEADQUARTERS, ARMY OF THE POTOMAC,
March 16, 1862.

Brigadier-General James S. Wadsworth, Military Governor of the District of Columbia:

SIR: The command to which you have been assigned, by instruction of the President, as Military Governor of the District of Columbia, embraces the geographical limits of the district, and will also include the city of Alexandria.

The defensive works south of the Potomac, from the Occoquan to Difficult Creek, and the part of Fort Washington. I enclose a list of the works and defences embraced in these limits. General Banks will command at Manassas Junction, with the divisions of Williams and Shields, composing the Fifth Army corps, but you should, nevertheless, exercise vigilance in your front, carefully guard the approaches in that quarter, and maintain the duties of advanced guards. You will use the same precautions on either flank. All troops not actually needed for the police of Washington and Georgetown, for the garrisons north of the Potomac, and for other indicated special duties, should be removed to the south side of the river. In the centre of your front you should post the main body of your troops, in proper proportions, at suitable distances, towards your right and left flanks. Careful patrols will be made to thoroughly scour the country in front, from right to left.

It is specially enjoined upon you to maintain the forts and their armaments in the best possible order, to look carefully after the instruction and discipline of their garrisons, as well as all other troops under your command, and by frequent and rigid inspection to insure the attainment of these ends.

The care of the railways, canals, depots, bridges and ferries within the above-named limits will devolve upon you, and you are to insure their security and provide for their protection by every means within your power. You will also protect the depots of the public stores and the transit of the stores to the troops in actual service.

By means of patrols you will thoroughly scour the neighboring country south of the eastern branch, and also on your right, and you will use every possible precaution to intercept mails, goods, and persons passing unauthorized to the enemy's lines.

The necessity of maintaining good order within your limits, and especially in the capital of the nation, cannot be too strongly enforced. You will forward and facilitate the movement of all troops destined for the active part of the army of the Potomac, and especially the transits of detachments to their proper regiments and corps.

The charge of all new troops arriving in Washington, and of all troops temporarily there, will devolve upon you. You will form them into provisional brigades, promote their instruction and discipline, and facilitate their equipments. Report all arrivals of troops, their strength, composition and equipment by every opportunity. Besides the regular report and returns which you will be required to render to the Adjutant-General of the Army, you will make to these headquarters a consolidated morning report of your command every Sunday morning, and a monthly return on the first day of each month.

The foregoing instructions are communicated by command of Major-General McClellan.

General McClellan made this masterly disposition of the forces specified by him; issued so complete and detailed instructions to the commanding officers, and presented so comprehensive a *resume* of all

HEADQUARTERS, ARMY OF THE POTOMAC,
March 16, 1862.

To Major-General N. P. Banks, commanding Fifth corps, Army of the Potomac:

SIR: You will post your command in the vicinity of Manassas, intrench yourself strongly and throw cavalry pickets well out to the front. Your first care will be the rebuilding of the railway from Washington to Manassas, and to Strasburg, in order to open your communications with the valley of the Shenandoah. As soon as the Manassas Gap Railway is in running order, intrench a brigade of infantry—say four regiments, with two batteries—at or near the point where that railway crosses the Shenandoah. Something like two regiments of cavalry should be left in that vicinity to occupy Winchester, and thoroughly scour the country South of the railway, and up the Shenandoah Valley, as well as through Chester Gap, which might, perhaps be occupied advantageously by a detachment of infantry, well intrenched. Block houses should be built at all the railway bridges occupied by grand guard, Warrenton Junction, or Warrenton itself, and also some still more advanced points on the Orange and Alexandria Railroad, as soon as the railroad bridges are repaired.

Great activity should be observed by the cavalry. Besides the two regiments at Manassas, another regiment of cavalry will be at your disposal, to scout towards the Occoquan, and probably a fourth towards Leesburg. To recapitulate, the most important points that should engage your attention are as follows:

First—A strong force, well intrenched, in the vicinity of Manassas, perhaps even Centreville, and another force. A brigade also well intrenched near Strasburg.

Second—Block houses at railway bridges.

Third—Constant employment of cavalry well to the front.

Fourth—Grand guards at Warrenton, and in advance as far as the Rappahannock if possible,

Fifth—Great care to be exercised to obtain full and early information as to the enemy.

Sixth—The general object is to cover the line of the Potomac and Washington.

The foregoing is communicated by order of Major-General McClellan.

HEADQUARTERS, ARMY OF THE POTOMAC,
STEAMER COMMODORE, April 1, 1862.

To Brigadier-General L. Thomas, Adjutant-General, U. S. A.:

GENERAL: I have to request that you will lay the following communication before the Honorable Secretary of War. The approximate numbers and positions of the troops left near, and in rear of the Potomac are about as follows:

General Dix has, after guarding the railroads under his charge, sufficient troops to give him five thousand men for the defence of Baltimore, and 1,988 available for the Eastern shore, Annapolis, &c. Fort Delaware is very well garrisoned by about four hundred men. The garrisons of the forts around Washington amount to ten thousand men, other disposable these to the Secretary of War, in the full belief that the words in the President's War Order, March 11, 1862,† meant what they

troops now with General Wadsworth being about eleven thousand four hundred men. The troops employed in guarding the various railroads in Maryland amount to some three thousand three hundred and fifty-nine men. These it is designed to relieve, being old regiments, by dismounted cavalry, and to send them forward to Manassas. General Abercrombie occupies Warrenton with a force which, including Col. Geary's at White Plains,, and the cavalry to be at their disposal, will amount to some seven thousand seven hundred and eighty men, with twelve pieces of artillery.

I have the honor to request that all the troops organized for service in Pennsylvania and New York, and in any of the Eastern States, may be ordered to Washington. This force I should be glad to have sent at once to Manassas—four thousand men from General Wadsworth to be ordered to Manassas. These troops, with the railroad guards above alluded to, will make up a force under the command of General Abercrombie to something like eighteen thousand six hundred and thirty-nine men. It is my design to push General Blenker from Warrenton upon Strasburg. He should remain at Strasburg long enough to allow matters to assume a definite form in that region before proceeding to his ultimate destination. The troops in the valley of the Shenandoah will thus—including Blenker's division, ten thousand and twenty-eight strong, with twenty-four pieces of artillery; Banks' Fifth corps, which embraces the command of General Shields, nineteen thousand six hundred and eighty-seven strong, with forty-one guns, some three thousand six hundred and fifty-three disposable cavalry, and the railroad guard, about twenty-one hundred men—amount to about thirty-five thousand four hundred and sixty-seven men.

It is designed to relieve General Hooker by one regiment—say eight hundred and fifty men—being, with five hundred cavalry, thirteen hundred and fifty men on the lower Potomac. To recapitulate: At Warrenton there is to be seven thousand seven hundred and eighty; at Manassas, say ten thousand eight hundred and fifty-nine; in the Shenandoah valley, thirty-five thousand four hundred and sixty-seven; on the Lower Potomac, thirteen hundred and fifty—in all, fifty-five thousand four hundred and fifty-six. There would then be left for the garrisons in front of Washington and under General Wadsworth some eighteen thousand men, exclusive of the batteries, under instructions. The troops organizing or ready for service in New York, I learn, will probably number more than four thousand. These should be assembled at Washington, subject to disposition where their services may be most needed. I am, very respectfully, your obedient servant,

GEO. B. McCLELLAN, Major General Commanding.

THE PRESIDENT'S WAR ORDER No. 3.

† EXECUTIVE MANSION, WASHINGTON, March 11, 1862.

Major-General McClellan having personally taken the field at the head of the army of the Potomac, until otherwise ordered, is relieved from the command of the other military departments, he maintaining command of the department of the Potomac. Ordered, further, that the departments now under the respective commands of Generals Halleck and Hunter, together with so much of that under General Buell as lies west of a north and south line, drawn through Knoxville, Tenn., be consolidated and designated the Department of the Mississippi, and that, until otherwise expressed; and that the Secretary of War, during McClellan's absence on the Peninsula, would see to it that his orders and instructions were punctually executed. Limited means of transportation had compelled General McClellan to leave some 45,000 men, under McDowell, and not included in the 70,000 men enumerated, and left under command of Generals Banks and Wadsworth respectively; near Alexandria, to embark on the return of the vessels in which the rest of the army had gone to the Peninsula. General McDowell's corps was selected as the one to bring up the rear, because, says General McClellan he wanted to use this corps as a unit for a movement in the rear of the enemy's fortifications on the left bank of the York river.

McClellan had hardly proceeded a few miles on his way to Fortress Monroe when, presto! presto! the President and the Secretary of War overthrew McClellan's plans completely, and without notifying him of it, prevent General McDowell from following the army of the Potomac to the Peninsula; detached General Banks and General Wadsworth from his command, forming an independent department for each of them, and thereby with one foul blow crippled the army under McClellan on the Peninsula, by depriving it of about one-third of its numerical strength; prevented the proper disposition of troops for the protection of the City of Washington, and destroyed the most perfect strategical combination for the capture of Richmond, and the termination of the war.

On the 9th day of April† President Lincoln accuses McClellan of having omitted and neglected certain military arrangements, while

ordered, Major-General Halleck have command of said department. Ordered, also, that the country west of the Department of the Potomac, and east of the Department of the Mississippi, be a military department to be called the Mountain Department, and that the same be commanded by Major-General Fremont. That all the commanders of Departments, after the receipt of this order by them respectively, report severally and directly to the Secretary of War, and that prompt, full, and frequent reports will be expected of all and each of them.

ABRAHAM LINCOLN.

† WASHINGTON, April 9, 1862.

To Major-General McClellan:

MY DEAR SIR: Your dispatches, complaining that you are not properly sustained, while they do not offend me, pain me very much. Blenker's Division was withdrawn before you left here, and you know the pressure under which I did it, and as I thought, acquiesced in it, certainly not without reluctance. After you left I ascertained that less than 20,000 unorganized men without a field battery, were all you designed should be left for the defence of Washington and Manassas Junction, and part of this,

McClellan's report, April 1st, to Adjutant-General Thomas, not only states, all the President declares neglected, to have been done; but while the specified number of men, of horses, and of artillery, left at the various places designated, and the entire report show the perfect manner in which the force of 73,400 men, including 77 pieces of artillery have been disposed to protect Washington and its approaches, all of which is corroborated by General William Barry's letter,* Dec. 10, 1862.

---

even, was to go to General Hooker's old position. General Banks' corps, once designed for Manassas Junction, was divided and tied up on the line of Winchester and Strasburg, and could not leave that position without again exposing the Upper Potomac and the Baltimore and Ohio Railroad.

This presented, or would present, when McDowell and Sumner should be gone, a great temptation for the enemy to turn back from the Rappahannock and sack Washington. My explicit directions that Washington, sustained by the judgment of all the commanders of corps, should be left secure, had been entirely neglected. It was precisely this that drove me to detain McDowell. I do not forget that I was satisfied with your arrangement to leave Banks at Manassas Junction. But when that arrangement was broken up, and nothing was substituted for it, of course I was not satisfied. I was constrained to substitute something for it myself. And now allow me to ask you, do you really think I could permit the line from Richmond via Manassas Junction to this city, to be entirely open, except what resistance could be presented by less than 20,000 unorganized troops? This a question which the country will not allow me to evade.

There is a curious mystery about the number of troops now with you. I telegraphed you on the 6th, saying that you had over 100,000 with you. I had just obtained from the Secretary of War a statement taken, as he said, from your own returns, making 108,000 then with you, and en route to you. You now say you will have but 85,000 when all en route to you shall have reached you. How can this discrepancy of 35,000 be accounted for? As to General Wool's command, I understand it is doing precisely what a like number of your own would have to do if that command was away.

And once more let me tell you, it is indispensable to you that you strike a blow. I am powerless to help. This you will do me the justice to remember, I was always opposed to going down the Bay in search of a field, instead of fighting at or near Manassas, as only shifting and not surmounting a difficulty; that we would find the same enemy and the same or equal intrenchments at either place. The country will not fail to note —is noting now—that the present hesitation to move upon an intrenched enemy is but the story of Manassas repeated.

I beg leave to assure you that I have never written or spoken to you in greater kindness of feeling than now, nor with a fuller purpose to sustain you so far as in my most anxious judgment I consistently can. But you must act. Yours very truly, A. LINCOLN.

---

* HEADQUARTERS, INSPECTOR OF ARTILLERY,
WASHINGTON, Dec. 10, 1862.

Major-General McClellan, United States Army:

GENERAL: It having been stated in several public prints, and in a speech of Senator Chandler of Michigan, in his place in the United States

This letter of the President, in our opinion, solves the mystery of the complete failure of the campaign of 1862.

Lieutenant-General Winfield Scott, after the disaster of Bull Run the first, said he ought to have been cashiered by President Lincoln, for having proved himself a coward, in yielding to the pressure brought to bear upon him, having, against his own better judgment, permitted McDowell to advance on Manassas. When he left Washington for Europe, the veteran hero's last advice to General McClellan was, *"Never permit any power to override your own well considered opinions."*

General Scott was weighed down by old age, an invalid, from wounds received in his country's battles, confined to a sick bed, when he yielded. Never before had he planned a grand campaign with his headquarters in Washington; besieged by the Congress of the United States. He had never had to deal with so many strategists by intuition.

Mr. Lincoln had the experience of General Scott before him; he had seen the old hero shed tears of sorrow and self-condemnation for his cowardice, in the face of his country's enemies. He had McClellan commended to him by General Scott, in the strongest terms, to rely

---

Senate quoting what he stated to be a portion of the testimony of Brigadier General Wadsworth, Military Governor of Washington, before the joint Senate and House committee "on the conduct of the War," that Major-General McClellan had left an insufficient force for the defence of Washington, and *"not a gun on wheels,"* I have to contradict this charge as follows, from the official reports made at the time to me (the Chief of the Army of the Potomac), and now in my possession, by the commanding officer of the Army of the light artillery troops left in camp, in the city of Washington, by your order. It appears that the following named field batteries were left:

Battery C, First New York artillery, Captain Barnes, two guns.
Battery K, First New York artillery, Captain Crounse, six guns.
Battery D, Second New York artillery, Captain Robinson, six guns.
Ninth New York Independent battery, Captain Shertonty, six guns.
Sixteenth New York Independent battery, Captain Locke.
Battery A, Second battalion New York Artillery, Captain Hogan, six guns.
Battery B, Second battalion New York Artillery, Captain McMahon, six guns.
Total, seven batteries, thirty-two guns.

With the exception of a few horses, which could have been procured from the Quartermaster's Department in a few hours, the batteries were all fit for immediate service, excepting the Sixteenth New York battery, *which, having been previously ordered on General Wadsworth's application to report to him for special service,* was unequipped with guns or horses. I am, General, very respectfully, your obedient servant,

WILLIAM F. BARRY.
Brigadier-General Inspector of Artillery, United States Army.

upon. He had seen in what masterly manner he had organized a large army.

McClellan, as General-in-Chief; in all matters concerning the movements of the army, was his only constitutional adviser.

With the vigor of manhood, with a prospect to immortalize himself if he, as a patriot, constitutionally fulfilled his high trust; with all this to sustain, to steel him, and to give him strength and firmness in his duty towards the army, Mr. Lincoln is compelled to write to McClellan, "Blenker's division was withdrawn before you left here, and you know *the pressure under which I did it*, and, as *I thought*, acquiesced in it."

He thereby proves that at the very beginning of the campaign, the Commander-in-Chief of the army and navy of the United States (as General Hitchcock testifies in the court of inquiry) was manifestly under great anxiety; that at the Department he discussed the disposition to be made of part of the army, with unmilitary, irresponsible chiefs of bureaus; that he submitted the plan for the campaign, made by the General-in-chief, to the discussion and approval of his subordinate officers,—thereby destroying discipline in the army—that he yielded to unconstitutional pressure; that he did that for which Winfield Scott had sentenced himself to be cashiered.

The Commander-in-Chief destroyed the plans prepared by the General-in-Chief; he gave to that General detailed orders in matters of which he had no knowledge;—he lost his head. As the Commander-in-Chief was unconstitutionally pressed right or left, forward or backward, so was our brave army, unmilitarily sent forward to-day and recalled to-morrow; moved to the East now, and ordered West the day after. The Commander-in-Chief thus prevents the success in the field, which the President declares to be necessary before anything else.

The telegraphic orders and instructions from the Commander-in-Chief, and from the Secretary of War to General McDowell, with that General's replies and reports thereto—the President's letter to McClellan, of April 9th—all his other letters published at the court, but in particular the Secretary of War's letter of *military instructions*, May 17, 1862,† to Major-General McClellan, in the face of Mc-

---

† SECRETARY STANTON TO GENERAL M'DOWELL.

WAR DEPARTMENT, April 11, 1862.

Major-General McDowell, Commanding:

SIR—For the present, and until further orders, you will consider the national capital as especially under your protection, and make no movement throwing your force out of position for the discharge of this primary duty.

EDWIN M. STANTON, Secretary of War.

Clellan's orders of March 16th, and April 1st, and of McDowell's telegraphic remonstrances—show a degree of unprincipled misrepresen-

GENERAL M'DOWELL TO THE PRESIDENT.

HEADQUARTERS, DEPARTMENT OF THE RAPPAHANNOCK, }
OPPOSITE FREDERICKSBURG, May 24, 1862. }

HIS EXCELLENCY THE PRESIDENT:

I obeyed your order immediately; for it was positive and urgent, and, perhaps, as a subordinate, there I ought to stop; but I trust I may be allowed to say something in relation to the subject, especially in view of your remark that everything depends upon the celerity and vigor of my movements. I beg to say that co-operation between General Fremont and myself to cut off Jackson and Ewell is not to be counted upon, even if it is not a practicable impossibility; next, that I am entirely beyond helping distance of General Banks, and no celerity or vigor will be available so far as he is concerned; next, that by a glance at the map it will be seen that the line of retreat of the enemy's forces up the valley is shorter than mine to go against him. It will take a week or ten days for the force to get to the valley by the route which will give it food and forage, and by that time the enemy will have retreated. I shall gain nothing for you there and lose much for you here. It is, therefore, not only on personal grounds that I have a heavy heart in the matter, but I feel that it throws us all back, and from Richmond north we shall have all our large mass paralyzed, and shall have to repeat what we have just accomplished.

I have ordered General Shields to commence the movement to-morrow morning. A second division will follow in the afternoon. Did I understand you aright that you wish that I personally should accompany this expedition?

Very respectfully, IRVIN M'DOWELL.

THE PRESIDENT TO GENERAL M'DOWELL.

WASHINGTON, May 24, 1862.

Major General McDowell:

I am highly gratified by your alacrity in obeying my orders. The change was as painful to me as it can possibly be to you or to any one. Everything now depends upon the celerity and vigor of your movements.

A. LINCOLN.

GENERAL M'DOWELL TO SECRETARY STANTON.

HEADQUARTERS, DEPARTMENT OF THE RAPPAHANNOCK, }
May 24, 1862. }

Hon. E. M. Stanton, Secretary of War:

The President's order has been received and is in progress of execution. This is a crushing blow to us.

IRVIN McDOWELL, Major-General.

THE PRESIDENT TO GENERAL M'DOWELL.

WASHINGTON, May 24, 1862.

Major-General McDowell:

General Fremont has been ordered, by telegraph, to move to Franklin and Harrisonburg, to relieve General Banks, and capture or destroy Jackson and Ewell's forces. You are instructed, laying aside for the present the movement on Richmond, to put twenty thousand men in motion

tation, self-conceit, vaccillation and military imbecility, as never before disgraced men, controlling the armies of a great nation, engaged in a struggle for life and death.

---

at once for the Shenandoah, moving on the line, or in advance of the line, of the Manassas Gap Railroad. Your object will be to capture the force of Jackson and Ewell, either in co-operation with General Fremont, or, in case want of supplies or transportation interfered with his movement, it is believed that the force which you move will be sufficient to accomplish the object alone. The information thus far received here makes it probable that, if the enemy operates actively against General Banks, you will not be able to count upon much assistance from him, but may have even to release him. Reports received this moment are that Banks is fighting with Ewell, eight miles from Harper's Ferry.

ABRAHAM LINCOLN.

WAR DEPARTMENT,
WASHINGTON, CITY, D. C., May 17, 1862.

Major-General George B. McClellan, Commanding Army of the Potomac, before Richmond:

Your dispatch to the President, asking for reinforcements, has been received and carefully considered. The President is not willing to uncover the capital entirely, and it is believed that even if this were prudent, it would require more time to effect a junction between your army and that of the Rappahannock, by the way of the Potomac and York rivers, than by a land march.

In order, therefore, to increase the strength of the attack upon Richmond at the earliest possible moment, General McDowell has been ordered to march upon that city by the shortest route. He is ordered—keeping himself always in position to cover the capital from all possible attack—so to operate as to put his left wing in communication with your right, and you are instructed to co-operate so as to establish this communication as soon as possible. By extending your right wing to the north of Richmond, it is believed that this communication can be safely established, either north or south of the Pamunkey river. In any event you will be able to prevent the main body of the enemy's forces from leaving Richmond, and falling, in overwhelming force, upon McDowell. He will move with between thirty-five and forty thousand men.

A copy of the instructions to Major-General McDowell are with this. The specific task assigned to his command has been to provide against any danger to the capital of the nation. At your earnest call for reinforcements, he is sent forward to co-operate in the reduction of Richmond, but charged, in attempting this, not to uncover the city of Washington, and you will give no orders, either before or after your junction, which can keep him out of position to cover this city. You and he will communicate with each other by telegraph or otherwise, as frequently as may be necessary for efficient co-operation.

When General McDowell is in position on your right, his supplies must be drawn from West Point, and you will instruct your staff officers to be prepared to supply him by that route.

The President directs that General McDowell retain the command of the Department of the Rappahannock, and of the forces with which he moves forward.

By order of the President,
EDWIN M. STANTON, Secretary of War.

Mr. Edwin M. Stanton orders Major-General McClellan, then at the head of a large army, in the field—among other things—"to use

THE INSPECTOR-GENERAL OF THE ARMY TO GENERAL MCDOWELL.

WASHINGTON, April 30, 1862.

Major-General McDowell, commanding Department Rappahannock:

GENERAL:—The Secretary of War has given me authority to inform you that you can occupy Fredericksburg with such force as in your judgment may be necessary to hold it for defensive purposes, but not with a view to make a forward movement. H. VAN RENSSELAER,
Inspector-General United States Army.

SECRETARY STANTON TO GENERAL MCDOWELL.

WASHINGTON, April 23, 1862.

Major-General McDowell, Aquia Creek:—

The President directs that you should not throw your force across the Rappahannock at present, but that you should get your bridges and transportation all ready and wait further orders.

EDWIN M. STANTON, Secretary of War.

SECRETARY STANTON TO GENERAL MCDOWELL.

WASHINGTON, May 24, 1862.

Major-General McDowell:—

In view of the operations of the enemy on the line of General Banks, the President thinks that the whole force you designate to move from Fredericksburg should not be taken away, and he therefore directs that one brigade, in addition to the one designated to leave at Fredericksburg, should be left there—this brigade to be the least effective of your command. EDWIN M. STANTON, Secretary of War.

GENERAL M'DOWELL TO GENERAL MCCLELLAN.

HEADQUARTERS, DEPARTMENT OF THE RAPPAHANNOCK,
MANASSAS, June 12, 1862.

Major-General G. B. McClellan, Commanding Department of Virginia, before Richmond:

The delay of Major-General Banks to relieve the division of my command in the valley beyond the time I had calculated on, will prevent my joining you with the remainder of the troops I am to take below, at as early a day as I named. My third division (McCall's) is now on the way. Please do me the favor to so place it that it may be in a position to join the others as they come down from Fredericksburg. IRVIN McDOWELL,
Major-General Commanding.

GENERAL M'DOWELL TO GENERAL MCCLELLAN.

June 10, 1862.

Major General McClellan. Commanding Department of Virginia, before Richmond:

For the third time I am ordered to join you, and hope this time to get through. In view of the remarks made with reference to my leaving you, and not joining you before, by your friends, and of something I have heard as coming from you on that subject, I wish to say I go with the greatest satisfaction, and hope to arrive with my main body in time to be of service. McCall goes in advance by water. I will be with you in ten days, with the remainder, by Fredericksburg. IRVIN McDOWELL,
Major-General Commanding.

the 'corps d'armee' under General McDowell, after it shall have reached Hanover Court House—140 miles from Washington—for the *reduction of Richmond*; but in attempting this, not to issue any orders which can lead General McDowell out of position to *cover the City of Washington.*"

We wanted testimony, given in open court, to the identity of the above letter before we believed it possible that any person outside a lunatic asylum could give such *instructions*.

Against the talent, skill, and strategical combinations of the most experienced and most daring of the Confederate generals, with their large armies, intelligently and heartily supported by their government, General McClellan and his gallant army, forsaken by the administration, had, in the seven days' battle, defeated them all, had accomplished what they considered impossible to be done; because in strategy and in tactics it eclipsed anything recorded in history.* The Army of the Potomac had at Harrison's Landing gained an impregnable position, and the only strategical base for a successful attack upon Richmond; which to move to at the outset, McClellan was prevented by the Merrimac's undisturbed control over the James River.

The army was here preparing for a new movement against the rebel capital, and waiting for recruits to fill up the ranks of the old regiments, and for reinforcements by other corps; when Major-General Halleck, the newly-appointed General-in-Chief of the armies of the United States, visited General McClellan's head-quarters from July 24th to 27th. Very soon after, the army of the Potomac was withdrawn from Harrison's Landing and from the Peninsula, and although this dangerous movement was accomplished in the most masterly manner and without the loss of a single man, it has, nevertheless, been declared by the strategists of all nations to be the most unpardonable strategical blunder committed, so far, during this war.

The principal object of the campaign of 1862, it must not be lost sight of, had been aggressive operation against the rebellion in general, and against Richmond, for its capture, in particular. Aggressive warfare had been demanded by the people and by Congress; it could hardly be undertaken early enough to satisfy this universal demand; for this purpose the administration had asked, and had received, with unexampled liberality, men and means ample in every respect. The government had ordered aggression, and General McClellan had

---

* For a detailed description of these battles, see "George B. McClellan from August, 1861, to August, 1862." N. Y., H. Dexter, 113 Nassau st.

planned everything in the most perfect manner to accomplish that distinctly stated object.

General Halleck, although far West, could not help being fully aware of this. In his report the General says of his visit to headquarters: " *The main object of this consultation was to ascertain if there was a possibility of an advance upon Richmond from Harrison's Landing, and if not, to form some plan of uniting the armies of General McClellan and General Pope on some other line.*"

General Halleck cannot for a moment have doubted the *possibility* to advance upon Richmond from Harrison's Landing; that possibility existed then and exists now. The General wants to say, we think, he went to consult with General McClellan what reinforcements he needed to insure the capture of Richmond; because the General at once says : " *I took the President's* ESTIMATE *of the largest number of reinforcements that could be sent to the Army of the Potomac ;*" and, besides, he nowhere states, or even *insinuates*, that he discovered *it to be impossible to advance upon Richmond from Harrison's Landing.* Thus considering the question of reinforcements, the principal and fundamental one, how does General Halleck proceed—he bases his action in this the most important operation in the war, the first one he is called upon to perform in his new office (to which he has been appointed undoubtedly with the object to obviate the grievous and ruinous blunders resulting from the mismanagement of military affairs by unmilitary men), he bases his decision in this matter—almost of life and death to the nation—upon the *estimate* of the President, of the very unmilitary man who, by his *false estimates* of the enemy's strength and intentions, and of his own ability to comprehend and direct military movements and matters, had materially contributed to the destruction of the army of General Banks, to the uselessness of General McDowell's army, and to the dangerous complications on the Peninsula, from which General McClellan had so miraculously extricated his army. He bases it upon this estimate, although a few hour's careful investigation of his own, would have convinced him that the President's *estimate* was far from the mark, would have shown that of the 300,000 men called for by the President (July 2d), thousands of new volunteers were daily placed at the disposal of the government. Pending the entire discussion of this matter of reinforcement, he does not state that he ever took the pains to ascertain *for himself* what forces there were disposable; but against the most conclusive argument of the ablest general in the nation, that his orders, if carried out will be disastrous to the best interests of the country; he always rests upon the *estimates* of a third person. When it finally appeared that General McClellan considered a reinforcement of 35,000, ten thousand less than under McDowell had been taken from him, necessary to insure the occupation of Richmond; when General McClellan had explained to him how futile all attempts must be against Richmond from other directions, how the heart of the rebellion is at Richmond, how one effective blow struck there will accomplish what cannot be accomplished anywhere else by ever so many blows, even then General Halleck does not survey the entire field of his resources himself, and overlooks— what afterward occurs to him—that there is a corps under General Cox in Western Virginia which can easily be spared, to supply the same number of men sent from Pope's army at Fredericksburgh to Harrison's Landing, which with General Burnside's corps and ten thousand more of Pope's army—the rest of which ought to have been withdrawn to the fortifications near Washington—would have amounted to 35,000 men and would have given us Richmond.

When, resting upon this vague estimate, the General arrived at the false conclusion that he cannot send 35,000 men to General McClellan, he thinks "*the only alternative now left was to withdraw the Army of the Potomac to some position where it could unite with that of General Pope, and cover Washington at the same time that it operated against the enemy.*" Although General Wadsworth had an army of over 20,000 men behind strong entrenchments in and near Washington; *although* that city was in no manner menaced by the enemy; *although* General Pope, with about 40,000 men, was near that city with no other reasonable object in view but to form an army of observation and protection around the national capital—General Halleck, by his ill-advised decision, changes the aggressive operations against the rebel capital, *which formed the basis of the entire campaign*, to a strategy of *defense*, for which he has to draw the attacking forces from the enemy's capital, at once relieved by this unparalelled strategical blindness.

We say that General Halleck drew the attacking enemy from before Richmond because his statement that about the 3d of August, "*he received information that the enemy was preparing a large force to drive back General Pope, and attack either Washington or Baltimore, which gave him uneasiness for the safety of the capital and Maryland, and I repeatedly urged upon General McClellan the necessity of moving his army. The evacuation of Harrison's Landing, however, was not commenced till the* 14*th, eleven days after it was ordered."**

The impression which General Halleck endeavors to create, that on the strength of "*the information he received*" he ordered the junction between the two armies, is flatly contradicted by the evidence under oath in the Porter court-martial, where it is distinctly stated, that on 20th day of August, when General McClellan was at Fortress Monroe and General Porter was at Newport News, the first information was received of movements from Richmond toward the Rappahannock; that, in other words, General Lee did not stir a man from Richmond till General Halleck by the withdrawal of McClellan made for him the opportunity. Even if the evidence of this fact had not been furnished by the court-martial, a cursory reading of General Halleck's Report shows that it contains as strong a self-contradiction of the insinuation made by its author.

If General Halleck learned and believed, before he ordered the junction, that Lee was about to advance with his whole force on General Pope, he would have ordered General McClellan to remain at Harrison's Landing—to advance on and take Richmond the moment Lee had left; then turn round, cut off Lee's supplies, attack him in the rear, and crush him between his own army and that of Pope. In the attempt of concealing the truth, the General-in-Chief stands self-accused, either of a stupidity unpardonable in a drummer boy, or of a determination to leave Richmond in possession of the rebels rather than that General McClellan should have the honor of its capture.

We look in vain over the report of the General-in-Chief for an explanation, why he directed the forces from the peninsula, when finally he ordered their withdrawal to Aquia Creek, and not to Alexandria. The army of General Pope, which to strengthen was General Halleck's object, while he intended to cover Washington also, was between Sperryville and Warrenton Junction; this position could be reached from Alexandria, with its spacious wharves and railroad facilities, by railroad in by far shorter a time, say three or four days, than of necessity it took the same forces to disembark at Aquia Creek, which possessed none of the facilities above alluded to, whence the troops had a longer march over ordinary roads; and while this march lasted were completely unavailable for the protection of the

---

* The definite order of General Halleck is dated August 6th, therefore the evacuation on the 14th was only eight days after it.

city of Washington; while on the road from Alexandria, per Fairfax, Manassas Junction, and so forth, they were always between the enemy's forces, if there were any, en route for the Capitol, or Washington. The mistake made in the selection of Aquia Creek is a further proof that the General-in-Chief's plan was ill-considered in the arrangements for its execution, as it was unjustifiable in its conception.

After a very detailed and minute description, of the lamentable campaign under General Pope,* (almost a verbatim extract of a long report by General Pope, September 3, 1862, to which the General alludes as Exhibit No. 4, but which is not published with this report,) of the credit for which the General-in-Chief claims a considerable share, he says, " Although this short and active campaign was, from causes already referred to,† less successful than we had reason to expect, it had accomplished *the great and important object of covering the Capitol* till troops could be collected for the defence." In the report of September 3d, 1862, dated, Headquarters Army of Virginia, (without stating where they are,) General Pope distinctly states at the *commencement, that the object of his campaign*, according to the instructions received at Washington, has been to draw the rebel army under Lee away from Richmond to the Rappahannock, and thereby to enable the army of the Potomac to leave Harrison's Landing, and be saved from utter destruction; towards the close of his report, he congratulates himself and the army of Virginia on the successful accomplishment of this object. With both the reports before us, and considering that General Halleck does not dispute General Pope's official statement to the General-in-Chief himself, we must say, either, one or the other of the two authors perverts the truth; or the General-in-Chief drew the rebel army intentionally from Richmond to Washington for the great and important object *of afterwards covering that city with the army under Pope against capture*.

But in this object, which he states has been accomplished, every-

---

* See page 31 to 45, Part I.

† General Halleck says : " *For some unexplained reason, General Porter did not comply with this order of General Pope, and his corps was not in the battles of the 28th and 29th.*" For this so-called unexplained reason of non-compliance with the order of General Pope, the latter presented charges against General Porter, and a court-martial convened in the city of Washington gave General Porter an opportunity to prove that *it was a physical impossibility* to execute the order of General Pope. The Judge Advocate, after all the evidence was in, had not a word to sustain any of the charges.

body knows General Halleck signally failed, so much so that he had officially to declare, although he does not say so in his report, *that it was impossible to save Washington from invasion by Lee's army* except by giving the entire command to General McClellan.

In his letter from Berkley, Virginia, August 4, 12 M., General McClellan indicates to the General-in-Chief—as far as in his position he has a right to do—the only wise plan of operations, that is, to withdraw half of Pope's army to a strict defence of the city of Washington, n case that should be menaced, and to send the rest, with Burnside, and all other troops he designates, to Harrison's Landing; because, said he, "*here is the true defence of Washington; it is here on the bank of the James River that the fate of the Union should be decided*," which is just as true to-day as it was on the 4th of August. General Halleck is not justified in saying in reply to this letter, referring to his plan of uniting the two armies, "*only one feasible plan has been presented for doing this. If you or any one else had presented a better one, I certainly should have adopted it.*" In the first place, it is the business of the General-in-Chief to devise the plan; in the second place, General McClellan had not only suggested the only good plan, but has, in detail, explained it. General Halleck either could not or would not understand it. Four short weeks after McClellan had explained it to the General-in-Chief, and had done so in vain, he proved by its practical execution how good a plan it was.

When he had only a portion of the old army left yet, and that, deprived of some of his best generals, and when the enemy, flushed with victory, was near Washington, and actually threatening it, General McClellan left a force about equal to half of Pope's last army of Virginia for its defence, and with the rest he whipped Lee out of Maryland, saved Washington and Baltimore at Antietam, and wiped away in Maryland the shame of Halleck and Pope in Virginia, which feat is hardly noticed in General Halleck's report.

Thus we see, when the direct interference of President and Seretary of War with the well-matured plans of General McClellan, *retarded* their execution and *increased* the work, hardships, and the sufferings of the army, that General Halleck, although he was told by General McClellan what would be the consequences, in his reckless ambition and conceit, in one mad order actually annulled the entire object of the campaign, and undid all that been done in its execution.

Cedar Mountain, Gainesville, Manassas, Bull Run, Chantilly, and other fields drenched with the blood of brave men, for which mother's

' tears never needed to have been shed; 35,000 in killed, wounded and prisoners, which, had he sent them to General McClellan, would have secured Richmond to us; the national capital again menaced by the foe ; the heart of rebellion saved and snatched from the grasp of our army ; years added to a already long war at a million dollars per day—all this we charge as a part of the result of the immeasurable military imbecility of the General-in-Chief, that led him in the face of the fullest argument, to annul the wise plan and override the counsel of George B. McClellan.*

---

* EXBIBIT NO. 1—A COPY IN CYPHER.

BERKELEY, Va., August 4—12 M.

Major General Halleck, Commander-in-Chief:

Your telegram of last evening is received. I must confess that it has caused me the greatest pain I ever experienced, for I am convinced that the order to withdraw this army to Aquia Creek will prove disastrous in the extreme to our cause. I fear it will be a fatal blow. Several days are necessary to complete the preparations for so important a movement as this, and while they are in progress, I beg that careful consideration may be given to my statement. This army is now in excellent discipline and condition. We hold a debouche on both banks of the James River, so that we are free to act in any direction, and with the assistance of the gunboats, I consider our communication as secure.

We are 25 miles from Richmond, and are not likely to meet the enemy in force sufficient to fight a battle until we are fifteen to eighteen miles, which brings us practically within ten miles of Richmond. Our largest line of land transportation would be from this point twenty-five miles, but with the aid of the gunboats we can supply the army by water, during its advance, certainly to within twelve miles of Richmond, with land transportation all the way. From here to Fortress Monroe is a march of about seventy miles, for I regard it as impracticable to withdraw this army and its material, except by land. The result of the movement would thus be to march 145 miles to reach a point now only twenty-five miles distant, and to deprive ourselves entirely of the powerful aids of the gunboats and water transportation. Add to this the certain demoralization of this army, which would ensue, the terrible depressing effect upon the people of the North, and the strong probability that it would influence foreign Powers to recognize our adversaries ; and these appear to me sufficient reasons to make it my imperative duty to urge in the strongest terms afforded in our language, that this order may be rescinded, and that far from recalling this army, it be promptly reinforced to enable it to resume the offensive.

It may be said that there are no reinforcements available. I point to General Burnside's forces, to that of General Pope, not necessary to maintain for the strict defence in front of Washington and Harper's Ferry ; to those portions as the army of the West not required for a strict defence there. Here, directly in front of this army, is the heart of the rebellion. It is here that all our resources should be collected to strike the blow which will determine the fate of this nation. All points of secondary importance elsewhere should be abandoned, and every available man brought here. A decided victory here, and the military strength of the rebellion is crushed. It matters not what partial reverses we may meet elsewhere; *here is the true defence of Washington ; it is here on the bank of the James River, that the fate of the Union should be decided.*

The startling evidences of a studied attempt, by every sort of perversion of truths and half truths, and by the artful torsion of facts, to throw upon General McClellan the responsibility for the reverses and disasters, invited by General Halleck himself, unnecessarily and against the most earnest warning, had hardly ceased to form the principal subject of astonishment and discussion, when the news of General Burnside's ill-fated attempt to cross the Rappahanock at Fredericksburg, gave a fresh shock to the already trembling nation. The army of the Potomac was on the 14th November divided in three grand divisions under command of Major-General Sumner, Hooker and Franklin respectively* while Major-General Sigel had chief com-

---

Clear in my conviction of right, strong in the consciousness that I have ever been and still am actuated solely by love of my country, knowing that no ambitious or selfish motives have influenced me from the commencement of this war, I do now, what I never did in my life before, I entreat that this order may be rescinded. If my counsel does not prevail, I will, with a sad heart, obey your order to the utmost of my power, devoting to the movement, whatever skill I may possess, whatever the result may be, and may God grant that I am mistaken in my forebodings, I shall at least have the internal satisfaction that I have written and spoken frankly, and have sought to do the best in my power to arrest disaster from my country.

GEO. B. McCLELLAN, Maj.-Gen.

* This division of the army, and the appointment of the commanding Generals took place per order and in the name of General Burnside—that is, to conform to the well-established principle, that whatever concerns the army entrusted to a general has to be performed by him and in his name. The violation of this principle by the *Commander-in-Chief*, when per war order No. 2, March 11, 1862, he himself designated the generals to command the various corps of the army of the Potomac, as well as the divisions of which each corps should be composed, was the first petty malice practised against General McClellan.

GENERAL ORDER—No. 184.
HEADQUARTERS ARMY OF THE POTOMAC,
NEAR WARRENTON, Va., Nov. 14, 1862.

First—The organization of a portion of this army into three grand divisions is hereby announced. These grand divisions will be formed and commanded as follows:

The Second and Ninth corps will form the right grand division, and will be commanded by Major-General E. V. Sumner.

The First and Sixth corps will form the left grand division, and will be commanded by Major-General W. B. Franklin.

The Third and Fifth corps will form the centre grand division, and will be commanded by Major-General Joseph Hooker.

The Eleventh corps, with such other troops as may hereafter be assigned to it, will constitute a reserve force, under command of Major-General Sigel.

Assignments of cavalry and further details will be announced in future orders.

mand of all the reserves. It was then concentrated and rapidly moved toward Fredericksburg. General Sumner's grand division leading, arrived at Falmouth, opposite Fredericksburg, about the 18th of November; the other two grand divisions soon followed and took position—General Sumner on the right, General Franklin on the left, and General Hooker in the centre. Having put their artillery in position, the army on the 12th of December crossed the river under the protection of a dense fog, over six pontoon bridges, built during the day. On the 13th the troops formed in line of battle in an open plain within range of the enemy's masked infantry and artillery. They were led to attack a position naturally strong, and made impregnable by three tiers of entrenchments well mounted with heavy guns, which had never been reconnoitred by the commanding general. They were repulsed with the loss of about 12,000 men, without having reached the enemy's lines to damage them. On the left wing General Franklin had succeeded in repulsing a sallying party, and taken from them some 700 prisoners; but he was also forced to retreat to his original line of formation. The enemy did not permit us to remove our wounded from within a certain distance nearest to their lines, but did not molest our army during the night in and near Fredericksburg, which was completely controlled by the enemy's guns, as were, also the upper pontoon bridges. On the 14th, by a tacit understanding, hostilities ceased, and at midnight on the 14th, in one of the severest storms on record, the army of the Potomac recrossed the river, took up all the bridges without the least molestation on behalf of the enemy, and reached the left bank at 8 o'clock A. M. on the 15th of December. A few hundred stragglers who had not been aware of the retrograde movement, fell into the hands of the enemy.

Thus December 13, at midnight, closed, amidst a severe storm, the second act of the grand military tragedy begun in October, when General McClellan was forced, in execution of a miserable strategical idea, to cross the Upper Potomac; the first part of which concluded

---

Major-General Sigel will exercise all the powers in respect to his command above assigned as the commanders of the grand divisions.

The commanders of these grand divisions will retain with them their respective staffs.

Fourth—The senior officer of the Second, Third, Fifth and Sixth corps will take command of these corps, and will forward to these headquarters a list of recommendations of officers to fill their staffs.

Eighth—All orders conflicting with these are hereby rescinded.

By command of   Major-General BURNSIDE.
S. WILLIAMS, Assistant Adjutant General.

Nov. 7, at midnight, in a snow storm, by the arrival of General Buckingham at Reutertown.

Major-General Burnside, it has to be remembered, on more than one occasion, refused the command of the army of the Potomac, tendered him by one or the other of the men in power at Washington. Brave, honest, heroic soldier as he is, he had invariably declared that he well knew he was not capable for such a command. At the same time he expressed his conviction that General McClellan, before any body else, was the man for the highest command.

When on the 7th of November he received the President's order assigning the command of the army to him, he intended again to decline, and only accepted after a long deliberation with other officers, because his resignation before the enemy might produce an evil effect on the army just deprived of the Commander in whom they possessed unlimited confidence.

Whatever, therefore, has been contributed to the disastrous affair of Fredericksburg, by the shortcomings of General Burnside in experience, in foresight, in decision, in proper combination, and in tactics on so large a scale, has all to be charged against him who, without cause, removed from command the best qualified and most experienced general, and compelled Burnside to assume command.

Our high opinion of General Burnside as a noble, patriotic gentleman, and as a daring, heroic-officer, does not relieve us from the duty we owe to the country, to history, to military science, and to truth, to point out the errors and mistakes in the arrangement and in the execution of the movement against Fredericksburg.

To move the entire army from the line near Gordonville, we consider bad strategy, because it unmasked to the enemy our real intentions, and enabled him to meet us in full force well prepared; he moved on the shorter line, and could reach Fredericksburg in less time than our army.

The various propositions of Generals Sumner and Hooker respectively to cross the river with their corps above, and move on the right bank, in our opinion prove that there existed roads by which the entrenchments of the enemy could and ought to have been reconnoitered, and their strength ascertained, sufficiently to prevent the commanding general from an attempt to take them by an infantry attack in front. The evidence before the commission shows that no reconnoissance had been made.

A naturally strong position, strengthened by three tiers of entrenchments, each mounted with many long-range guns, supported by infantry behind breastworks, under command of an experienced general, a position approachable only over an open field about a mile and a half long, bordering on a river with an open low bank—such a position is a Malakoff, a Mont-martre—if it has to be taken at all, it can be taken only *a la* Malakoff, or *a la* Mont-martre, that is, with the spade—by a gradual approach in counter works, and with heavy artillery ; attacked in front by infantry alone, it will, in ninety-nine cases out of a hundred, prove a rock from which the attacking column will recoil crippled and bleeding, to be annihilated in its retreat to the river.

Such is the position occupied by the Confederate army near Fredericksburg, and because it is such, all the bravery of our gallant soldiers did not even enable us to learn from our own observation, how strong an army the enemy had in and around this position We think the attack, as directed by General Burnside, a great mistake, and the escape of his army almost miraculous.

The idea to break this line of entrenchments by an infantry charge in the hope of piercing it and then destroying the enemy, we consider erroneous.

Napoleon Bonaparte based his tactics of breaking the centre of the enemy's army—which he practised on open battle-fields only—upon the superior discipline, and the more perfect movability of the French army under his own command, which enabled him to whip the two parts of the broken hostile army separately, because one half of them would be, for a time, without a head, and the half that remained with the general-in-chief would be numerically inferior to his own army This principle is not applicable to a chain of entrenchments placed in succeeding tiers; here every entrenchment is a citadel in itself; in case the enemy should carry one, each of the rest has its own commander, and has lost only a comrade. The striking similarity between the rebel position at Fredericksburg and that at Cedar Mountain (the former on a larger scale) ought to have taught General Burnside the necessity of adopting a different plan. Had General Banks, at Cedar Mountain, not been able to put his excellent artillery in a position from which it did terrific execution upon the enemy's batteries, his entire army would have been destroyed.*

Not to attempt the building of a pontoon bridge in face of an enemy before the opposite bank has been cleared from the foe, is a rule as old as military science itself. This rule General Burnside did not

---

* See pages 36 and 37, Part I.

remember until after he had lost half a day, and many men of the most valuable troops in any army—most valuable, because they can be replaced with great difficulty. To send the unarmed engineer out upon the end of a bridge to be shot down by sharpshooters behind old buildings, is not war. The engineer regiments, in particular the Fifteenth New York Volunteers, have earned for themselves a glorious name; they had built the two bridges on the left wing, and enabled General Franklin to cross about noon; while the Fiftieth Regiment, engaged on the bridges on the right wing, had been unable to accomplish anything; the Fifteenth were sent for—with a cheer they set to work, and completed the bridge on the right—and so did the work of both.

The manner in which General Burnside concluded to carry out a certain plan of operations; and when remonstrated with by one or the other of his officers, becomes convinced that his plan was impracticable or deficient, had to be changed or altogether to be abandoned, shows that he is not possessed of that circumspection, foresight, and forethought indispensible in the commander of a large army.

That notwithstanding these errors, oversights and mistakes, the army crossed the river, and could, two days later, return to the left bank, is no evidence that these errors and mistakes were not committed.

General Franklin says: " For *some unaccountable* reason they (the rebels) allowed us to cross, and did not open their batteries." We can find but one plausible explanation why the enemy did not earnestly oppose the crossing of our army on the 12th.

The war has lasted longer than the people at large had expected, and the cry for a decisive battle had been heard ever since the battle of Antietam. When General Lee found that Burnside actually commenced to move his army to the right bank of the Rappahannock, we think he considered this his opportunity to satisfy the clamor for a decisive battle, and concluded to let our entire army cross under a faint resistance; sufficient to make us more eager to follow up the imaginary advantage; to repulse our first attack as mildly as it could be done; thereby inducing us to repeat it with *all* our forces; thus opening a space between our rear and the city for the purpose of throwing cavalry and infantry masses, from his extreme right and left, into our rear. while all his artillery opened on our front, and while his long-range guns destroyed our bridges in the centre and on our right. That, under such circumstances, Burnside's entire army would have either been destroyed or captured, cannot very well be doubted; the evidence of Generals Burnside, Sumner, and Hooker before the Investigating Committee proves that the first part of the above programme was carried out to the letter, and how near General Burnside came to carry out the second part designated to be performed by our army. The heavy rain and severe gale prevented the rebel army noticing the withdrawal of our army to Falmouth until it was accomplished, and presented to General Burnside the golden opportunity to save the rest of his noble army from certain death.

When the news of the fearful slaughter at Fredericksburg became known, the people with one voice said, *this is the fault of the administration at Washington—it is not Burnside's fault*. General Burnside thereupon had a letter to General Halleck published, wherein he exonerated everybody else from blame, and declared himself and alone responsible for the plan, for its execution, and for its failure. This letter, if genuine, does more credit to the brave Burnside's noble heart than to his head. How could he expect the army ever to have confidence in him as a leader after he openly admits to have committed so grave mistakes? It did not calm the excitement. Soldiers are the severest and the best judges of their officers, here as well as in every other country.

Thus, by the appointment of General Burnside to the chief command, against his better judgment, the country has lost an excellent commander of a corps, but has not found a fit General, another evidence how true it is that a good soldier at the head of a division makes a melancholy failure when placed beyond that.

The Senate Committee on the War thought proper to proceed to Falmouth and there to investigate the matter. This examination proves that General Burnside on the 9th of November, at the request of General Halleck, sent his plan of operations on Fredericksburg to Washington; that on the 4th of November the General-in-Chief, the Quartermaster-General and General Haupt visited him at his headquarters in Warrenton. There they discussed his plan in all its details, and it was agreed that General Burnside should at once make all preliminary arrangements for the immediate execution of the same, so that the moment it should receive the approval of the President, which General Halleck was to procure, the most speedy execution thereof should at once take place. General Halleck, at the headquarters of General Burnside, on the 12th of Nov., 7:10, P. M., issued a telegraphic order to General Woodbury at Washington *to have the pontoon and bridge material transported to Aquia Creek.** After his return to Washington the General-in-Chief saw the President, who approved Burnside's plan. General Halleck hereupon telegraphed to the latter *to go ahead as he had proposed.* General Burnside concentrated his army and moved Sumner's division to Falmouth, where this officer had to come to a dead halt, because the pontoons which he expected to find were *non est.* To the want of pontoons, without which the Rappahannock could not be crossed, all the general officers attribute the disastrous affair at Fredericksburg.

General Franklin says : I would like to impress as firmly upon the Committee as it is impressed upon my mind, that this whole disaster has resulted from the delay in the arrival of the pontoon bridges. *Whoever is responsible for that delay is responsible for all the disasters that have followed.* General Burnside testifies that he was under the impression that General Halleck who gave the orders for the pontoons to be sent to Aquia Creek, would see to it that this order was properly carried out; because otherwise he would have carried it out himself. General Woodbury testifies that he received Halleck's order—that he found it impossible to start the pontoons as early as was expected, and then says—General Halleck's order to me on the 13th made it apparent that the army was preparing to march on Fredericksburg. Fearing that the movement would be precipitate, I went to General Halleck's office and urged him to delay the movement some five days, in order that the necessary preparations might be made to insure success. To this he replied that he would do nothing to delay for an instant the advance of the army upon Richmond. I rejoined that my suggestions were not intended to cause delay, but rather to prevent it. General Halleck admits that he went to Warrenton, and there at length discussed General Burnside's plans; that he issued the order to General Woodbury to send the pontoons; that he told Burnside to made all preliminary preparations to execute his plans when approved; that he got the President's approval of Burnside's plans, and that he telegraphed to the latter *to go ahead as he had proposed.* That on his return to Washington he was called upon by General Woodbury and notified of the impossibility to move the

---

* WARRENTON, Nov. 12—7: 10 P. M.
Brigadier General WOODBURY, Engineer Brigade :—
 Call upon the Chief Quartermaster, Colonel Rucker, to transport all your pontoons and bridge materials to Aquia Creek. Colonel Belgor has been ordered to charter and send me one hundred barges to Alexandria.
 H. W. HALLECK, General-in-Chief.

pontoons as early as could be expected; but as to the direct request of Gen Woodbury to postpone the movement, and as to his reply thereto his recollection is indistinct. The General-in-Chief of the army tries to clear himself from the culpable neglect of duty with which he is charged in the above testimony, by saying—" that all the troops in and around Washington were under command of General McClellan; that he issued his orders direct to the commanding officer at Washington with one single exception; that the troops should be moved from the command of Washington until I was notified by Gen. McClellan or the commanding officer here (Washington.) *I was told that Burnside when he relieved McClellan stood in the same position.*"

We have before had occasion to see what, since September last, was the official position of General McClellan in relation to General Halleck; to see that the latter had no control, or authority, or interference whatever with the operations of General McClellan; in fact, to see that officially he did not know anything about them. This relation between them was one of the principal causes of McClellan's removal from command.

General Halleck by this part of the testimony wishes to show that he considered he had as little right to interfere with the army under General Burnside as when it was under General McClellan. *O that for Burnside's sake and the army this had been true!* That this was not the case, that the official relation between the General-in-Chief and General Burnside, at the head of the army of the Potomac, was as different from that between General McClellan and General Halleck as black is different from white. This is clearly shown by the very presence of General Halleck at Burnside's headquarters; by his asking Burnside to prepare a plan and to submit it to him; by his discussion of Burnside's plan and by his taking it to the President for approval.

General McClellan did not trust the General-in-Chief with the secret of his plan for the campaign, although the former over and over again asked him to let him know it; still less would he allow the least part in the execution thereof to be directed by General Halleck. When General Halleck communicated to General McClellan anything about the intended operations of the army, he did it only as *especially instructed by the President*, not as General Halleck. This self-contradiction prevents the General's acquittal on the plea that *officially he had nothing to do* with the general supervision of the operations of the army under General Burnside.

To the question—" Was there or not any agreement or understand-

":ng between you and General Burnside that the pontoons and any "stores necessary for him to cross the river and move toward Fred- "ericksburg, should be furnished to him by the authorities here, "(Washington,) without his looking after them himself?"—General Halleck answers, "*Yes, sir.* I told General Burnside that everything "was at his disposition. He must make his own requisitions and "give his own orders; that I would not interfere, *except to assist in* "*carrying his views out as much as I could; whenever anything was* "*reported to me as not being done that I would render all the assis-* "*tance in my power.*"

Here then is from his own mouth his promise to Burnside that he would assist in carrying out his views as much as he could, and when anything was " reported as not being done (as was reported by Gen. Woodbury) that he would render all assistance in his power." All this he promised in regard to orders given by General Burnside ; how much more was he in duty bound to do the some in regard to the order to General Woodbury, which he himself had issued.

General Halleck knew that General Burnside's view was to take Fredericksburg by surprise if possible; that therefore the time be- tween the arrival of the vanguard of his army in view of the city, and between its actual occupation, should be as short as possible; he must have known that the appearance and the halt of Burnside's army at Falmouth, would be the signal for the enemy to put up his defensive works. With this knowledge in his possession; forwarned by General Woodbury of the dangers which an arrival at Falmouth of the army, before the pontoons were there, was sure to involve ; asked to notify General Burnside of the impossibility to have the pontoons at Falmouth at a time when Burnside, (ignorant of the impediments) could reasonably expect their arrival—the General-in- Chief of the army *wantonly violates* his different promise to General Burnside, to "render him all the assistance in his power"—does not even give him a single notice of what officially and alone, *in conse-* *quence of the order to General Woodbury having been sent by Hal-* *leck*, has been reported to him and not to General Burnside. By this criminal willful omission he allows the army of the Potomac to be led to destruction, and thus becomes principally responsible for the lives of the 12,000 brave slaughtered soldiers.

We will not pause to dissect the atrocious indescribable meanness with which the General-in-Chief, after having deceived him with false expectations, which he knowingly disappointed, attempts to cast the blame of the failure on General Burnside. As an officer in the army of the United States, as the General-in-Chief of his army, General Halleck as well as any other officer and soldier, is in duty bound to give immediate information to the proper officers of everything, be it ever so trifling, that by any possibility can have any bearing upon the movements or operations of the army or any part thereof.

So universal is this duty enforced in all armies, that if, for instance, a single wagon of the pontoon train had, on the march, broken down near any of the pickets of our army, such an accident would have been immediately reported to the nearest officer, who would have been in duty bound to send this report to the place where the train had started, (Washington,) as well as to the point of its destination, (General Burnside's Headquarters); or had a scouting party passed the broken wagon they would have made a report to the nearest officer. The importance of this rule for the safety of an army is so self-evident, that we merely allude to it. The General-in-Chief's principal and first duty is a general supervision of the execution of the plans of the campaign; to procure *perfect concert of action* between all the distinct and separate corps and branches of the army designed to cooperate; to urge the slow to move more rapidly, and to hold back those that move too fast. Under this general duty of the General-in-Chief, General Halleck was *bound* to notify General Burnside *without a moment's delay*, of the impossibility to start the pontoons as early as the latter had a right to expect it. That General Halleck himself gave the order about the pontoons to General Woodbury direct, —that he impressed General Burnside with the belief that he also would see to its execution, and thereby caused him not to enquire any more about it—that by issuing the order himself he had induced General Woodbury to report the impossibility " *to start the pontoons at once,*" to General Halleck and *not* to General Burnside, (as he would have done, had the order to him been issued by the latter) and—Halleck's promise to Burnside " *that he would render him all the assistance in his power* "—all these circumstances aggravate the culpability of the General-in-Chief.

The private soldier who falls asleep when on picket duty and thereby omits to watch over the safety of the camp, suffers death, whether or no his neglect causes a surprise or capture of the camp; because of the bad example to the army and of the impossibility to preserve proper discipline if such neglect should be permitted to pass unpunished.

The intentional omission of the General-in-Chief to notify General Burnside—when expressly requested to do so by General Woodbury

—of the unavoidable delay in the start of the pontoons, upon which the operations of Burnside's army were based, constitutes a crime by far greater than many of those, under the articles of war punished with death. It caused the wholesale slaughter of 10,000 Union soldiers.

The discipline of the army, which constitutes its efficiency; the safety of the country; justice to the 10,000 slain on the bank of the Rappahannock; justice to their parents, their widows, their orphans; justice to those who may yet be called to fight their country's battles; justice to all demand that the Commander-in-Chief order Major-General H. W. Halleck to be tried before a court-martial on the charge of "*wilful neglect of duty which he was requested to fulfill—such neglect having caused the loss of* 10,000 *men, and the disastrous defeat of our army at Fredericksburg, December* 13, 1862."

On the 1st day of January, 1863, President Lincoln issued, in accordance with his proclamation of September 22, 1862, his so-called Emancipation Proclamation.

WASHINGTON, January 1.

BY THE PRESIDENT OF THE UNITED STATES OF AMERICA, A PROCLAMATION.

Whereas, on the twenty-second day of September, in the year of our Lord one thousand eight hundred and sixty-two, a proclamation was issued.

* * * * * * * *

Now, therefore, I, Abraham Lincoln, President of the United States, by virtue of the power in me vested as Commander-in-Chief of the Army and Navy of the United States in time of actual armed rebellion against the authority and government of the United States, and as a fit and necessary war measure for suppressing said rebellion, do, on this first day of January, in the year of our Lord one thousand eight hundred and sixty-three, and in accordance with my purposes so to do, publicly proclaimed for the full period of one hundred days, from the day first above-mentioned, order, designate, as the states and parts of states wherein the people thereof respectively are this day in rebellion against the United States, to wit:

ARKANSAS.

LOUISIANA—(Except the parishes of St. Bernard, Placquemines, Jefferson, St. John, St. Charles, St. James, Ascension, Assumption, Terre Bonne, Lourche, Ste. Maria, St. Martin, and Orleans, including the city of New Orleans.)

MISSISSIPPI,
ALABAMA,
FLORIDA,
GEORGIA,
SOUTH CAROLINA,
NORTH CAROLINA, and

VIRGINIA—(Except the forty-eight counties] designated as West Virginia, and also the counties of Berkley, Accomac, Northampton, Elizabeth City, York, Princess Ann, and Norfolk, including the cities· of Norfolk and Portsmouth, and which excepted parts are for the present left precisely as if this proclamation were not issued.)

And, by virtue of the power, and for the purpose aforesaid, I do order and declare that all persons held as slaves within said designated States and parts of States are, and henceforward shall be, FREE. And that the executive government of the United States, including the military and naval authorities thereof, will recognize and maintain the freedom of said persons.

And I hereby enjoin upon the people so declared to be free to abstain from all violence, unless in necessary self-defence, and I recommend to them that, in all cases when allowed, they labor faithfully for reasonable wages.

*   *   *   *   *   *   *   *

{ SEAL. } Done at the city of Washington this first day of January, in the year of our Lord, one thousand eight hundred and sixty-three, and of the Independence of the United States of America the eighty-seventh.

* ABRAHAM LINCOLN.

By the President,

WM. H. SEWARD, Secretary of State.

The President issues the above order by virtue of the power vested in him as Commander-in-Chief of the army and navy of the United States; that is in his capacity as Commander-in-Chief. (This order is countersigned by the Secretary of State, not by the Secretary of War.) In this capacity Mr. Lincoln is undoubtedly subject to the rules and usages applicable to the orders and actions of the Commanders-in-Chief of other armies, and he places himself on a par with them.

No orders of a commander have effect beyond the territory in actual possession of the armies under his command; nor beyond the time of such actual occupation.

The orders of a commander become effective only as far as he possesses the power at any moment to enforce them. The Commander-in-Chief of the army of the United States surrounds the territory wherein his war order sets forever free all the slaves, with a circle of slave States distinctly exempt from the operation thereof, and so makes it impossible for himself to enforce his order. The right to take private property from the inhabitants of the enemy's country is not recognized by the rules of civilized warfare.

When Napoleon Bonaparte had entered Russia Prince Poniatowski, an eminent Polish nobleman, is said to have suggested to him, how deadly a blow he could strike against Russia by issuing a decree liberating all the serfs. The emperor replied : "France would curse me were I to do it, because I would thereby give the Russians the right to rob every Frenchman of his private property, should they ever enter France; and, my friend, do not forget that I could not liberate the Poles till I occupied Poland, and therefore I cannot liberate the serfs, even were I inclined to do so, till I have occupied Russia." Napoleon's opinion in matters like this is entitled to respect.

The tendencies of the civilized world during the last two centuries have been to reduce as much as possible the so-called *war power*, upon which alone Mr. Lincoln bases his right to issue the proclamation; to reduce it in the interest of civilization and humanity. The excesses of the French in Algiers, and those of the English in India and in China, have called forth a cry of horror and indignation throughout Christendom; they were committed against foreign and half-barbarian *unchristian* nations. How insignificant would these excesses appear compared with the horrors of a servile insurrection of 3,000,000 Africans against our own erring brothers, with whom we are connected by thousands of family ties, and with whom we hope, one of these days, again to live in peace and harmony as one nation. The Commander-in-Chief apprehends such an insurrection, because he distinctly enjoins the slaves to abstain from it.

Whether this unholy war be continued for years to come, or whether the battle, Dec. 13, at Fredericksburg has been the last great battle; to the military world, the period from August 1861 to January 1863, will forever form a subject of intense interest, of the most scrupulous investigation and professional speculation; on account of the rapidity with which the Union army of about 450,000* men was put in the field; on account of the magnificent armament of every branch of this vast army, unequaled in any other country; on account of the —in so short a time—unheard-of expenditure of about $1,200,000,000, and the army not paid—one of the most demoralizing neglects to any army; in consideration of the fact that in General McClellan the nation has found a general whose genius and skill as a strategist and as a tactician, by competent judges of all nations is admitted to be unsurpassed by the most famous captains of any age, while in Generals F. J. Porter, Franklin, Sumner, Hooker, Heintzelman, Burnside, Rosecrans, Keys, Stoneman, Banks, Hancock, Sigel, and many others,

---

* We believe the future will show that the above number has, at no time during the war, been exceeded by all our armies actually under arms; all the Reports of the Secretary of War to the contrary notwithstanding.

we possess intelligent, competent, and brave commanders of *corps d'armee*;* on account of the undisputed bravery, endurance, and superior fighting qualities generally displayed by our army; on account of the little effect, as yet, produced upon the army by the corrupting influences to which, in almost every conceivable form, it has been subjected, and on account of the absence of any lasting advantage really gained by so large and expensive an army in so many hard-fought battles.

In justice to the loyal citizen-soldiers of the North—in justice to their military talent and application—in justice to their heroic bearing and endurance—we present to the military world the following brief record of the Union Army and their performances in Virginia and Maryland.

Mr. Lincoln, the Commander-in-chief of the Army and Navy, when the present war commenced entertained the erroneous idea that the *rebellion* could be suppressed within ninety days by a *posse-comitatus*; he called out 75,000 volunteers for ninety days; over-ruled General Scott's military advice, and sent those "ninety days" men, unorganized, into what was expected to be a *spectacle militaire* for the members of Congress and their friends, but what shaped itself into the disgraceful rout—Bull Run the First.

General McClellan was then placed in the command resigned by General Scott. In the capital, surrounded by the enemy's forces, he organized a new army, as it was best possible under existing circumstances. He prepared a plan for a campaign, contemplating the capture of Richmond and the suppression of the rebellion; a plan that, as proved by official documents lately come to light before the court-martials above referred to, was not only perfect in its strategical conception, but, if ever equalled, was certainly unsurpassed in detailed

---

* Among the few gratifying reflections called forth by this war, is the high standard of professional efficiency universally possessed by the officers graduated from the Military Academy at West Point; whether they have continuously held commissions in the United States Army, or whether, for a time, they had resigned, followed other callings in civil life, and had received new commissions at the outbreak of the present war. No military academy can endow the students with genius, nor turn out commanders-in-chief; generals able judiciously to command armies of 150,000 men or more, are born hardly once in a century: but the fact that almost all our present most able generals were majors or captains two years ago; the exemplary manner in which large funds passing through their hands are always properly accounted for without any loss to the country, place West Point, as a military educational institute, at a par, if not ahead of, similar institutions in any other country. There are exceptions, to be sure—that of General Halleck the most striking of all—but they are few and far between.

elaboration, in completeness, in its comprehensive ramifications, in its far-reaching anticipation of events, as well as in the necessary preparations to meet them.

This plan the general intended to keep secret till after the commencement of its practical execution; its success could be interfered with by the result of battles only. In conformity with his plan, the army of the West had commenced operations in the field; had been successful in every one of their numerous engagements from Somerset, Bowling Green, Fort Henry, to Columbus; when a few days before the army of the Potomac was to commence the execution of the part assigned to them, the President, Commander-in-Chief, officially ordered General McClellan to communicate to him his plan. The general had to obey orders. The Commander-in-Chief assured his enquiring friends that this time success was certain; he proved the correctness of his views by explaining the plan: a few hours later the Confederate General Johnson, at Manassas, knew the plan; he at once retreated with his army to Richmond. The friends of the Commander-in-Chief thereupon censured General McClellan for having allowed the escape of Johnson's army from Manassas.

The President, Commander-in-Chief, relieved General McClellan as General-in-Chief of the army, and assigned this position "de facto" to Mr. Edwin M. Stanton, Lawyer and Secretary of War, General McClellan embarked his army for the peninsula; on his arrival there he found that 45,000 men under General McDowell, by order of the Commander-in-Chief, had not been permitted to embark, and had been placed at the disposal of Mr. Edwin M. Stanton; that his most perfect disposition of the forces under Generals Banks, Wadsworth, Abercrombie and others, between the Rappahannock, the Shenandoah, and the Potomac, and especially in front of Washington, had all been countermanded by the Commander-in-Chief and Mr. Edwin M. Stanton.

The betrayal of McClellan's plan for the campaign to the enemy enabled the latter to concentrate his forces in positions heretofore undefended. This and the numerical deduction of 45,000 men from his army, considerably delayed the advance of the army on the peninsula.

The Commander-in-Chief's friends censured McClellan's slowness.

When the army of the Potomac was within a few miles of Richmond, General McClellan asked now to have restored to him the 45,000 men withheld from his army; they then stood within four days march of his present lines; the Commander-in-Chief did not permit them to rejoin McClellan's army.

The Confederate army at Richmond, largely reinforced from all parts of the Confederate States, hereupon attacked the army of the Potomac with the intention of destroying it by superiority of numbers and by advantage of position. By most sublime strategy, executed in the most perfect manner—by the heroic bravery of his officers and men, McClellan snatched from their combined efforts the victory, which the Confederate generals considered certain; he secured the admirable position at Harrison's Landing, and sent the rebel army that ventured to attack Malvern Hill badly whipped to Richmond.

A dozen battles the army of the Potomac had fought on the peninsula without having received any reinforcements; McClellan now asked for 35,000 men to replace the losses in battle and for the purpose of taking Richmond; he points out where there are such that can be spared; he explains the importance of taking Richmond now, and from Harrison's Landing, and he foretells the consequences of a neglect to do it.

In the face of all this, General H. W. Halleck, just appointed General-in-Chief, peremptorily orders General McClellan to remove his entire army from Harrison's Landing to Aquia Creek, a place from which the ostensible object of this movement can hardly be accomplished.

The President Commander's friends bitterly complain that by McClellan's fault and slowness, the campaign on the peninsula had not given Richmond to Mr. Lincoln, and that the expected results have not been achieved. Arriving at Aquia Creek, the army of the Potomac, in separate corps is, by the Commander-in-Chief, detailed to the command of General Pope, and McClellan finds himself stripped of command.

Ten days had hardly passed, however, before the Confederate General Lee, with his army, appears in front of Washington, driving the demoralized and defeated army of Mr. Pope before him.

Self-preservation now becomes law supreme with the President Commander; whether or no his friends and his advisers are a unit on that point. He himself is convinced that General McClellan alone can preserve him and his friends. He reinstates the general in his high command, who accepts only on a condition not to be interfered with by anybody. The President Commander agrees to this and promises to stick to it.

In two weeks McClellan fights the battles of South Mountain and of Antietam, drives General Lee out of Maryland back across the

Potomac, and finishes the campaign in Maryland. He now asks for shoes, clothing, and other necessaries, for the want of which the army suffers and cannot move; all his most urgent requests don't bring the shoes. The Commander-in-Chief's friends circulate rumors that there exists no want of shoes and clothing in the army and then find fault with McClellan, that he complains of an imaginary want, and the Secretary of War enters into an elaborate correspondence with the General-in-Chief for the purpose of proving that there exists no want in the army; they both signally fail in their object, but they prove their hostility against McClellan, the neglect of the War Department, and the want of rectitude in the General-in-Chief.

The President Commander's friends now censure McClellan severely, because he permits the army to lay still and allows the Confederate army to stop in the Shenandoah Valley.

In the mean time McClellan is maturing his plan for the new campaign. Remembering the betrayal in March last of his plans, to the enemy, he refuses to communicate it to anybody.

The President Commander thereupon in the latter part of October, forced General McClellan to cross the Upper Potomac, and to commence the execution of a miserable strategy, not his own. A few days later, when the entire army is face to face with the enemy, the President Commander again removes McClellan from command, assigning it to Major-General Burnside, but not assigning any reason for the removal. A few hours after the receipt of this order McClellan transfers his command, tells his army to "stand by Burnside as you stood by me," and departs. The President Commander's friends thereupon rejoice—they congratulate the President, themselves and the nation on the appointment of General Burnside as his successor, because they know him to be the man in whom the army reposes the greatest confidence, and who will they are sure, take Richmond before the first day of January next. Burnside himself declares over and over again that he is not competent to lead so large an army; that McClellan, whom he knows as he knows himself, is the best man to command, *because he has the soundest head and the clearest military perception of any man in the United States.* But Burnside is a soldier, and the President Commander's friends are not, therefore Burnside's opinion can have no weight against theirs in military matters.

People in England, in France and in Russia, who have had a Cromwell, two Napoleons and Striletzers are astonished. They wonder that McClellan, at the head of 150,000 men devotedly attached to him, surrounded by his friends, obeyed the order of the President, instead of marching to Washington and deposing him and his advisers. These people do not know the patriot McClellan.

General McClellan when in Washington planned and worked for his country's cause; when in the field he fought for that cause; when misrepresented and slandered, when degraded, he suffered for that cause. Whether in the tented field, or in the Cabinet, McClellan never lost sight of his country's cause; neither the President nor a General-in-Chief, nor all the members of the Cabinet could for an instant obstruct from his clear view, his country's cause. He conquered self and kept silent for his country's cause; but the most powerful orator's brilliant eloquence could not have better enlightened the people about our country's cause and its mismanagers, than George B. McClellan has done by his dignified silence.

May no inferior man ever have presented to him the same tempting opportunity and take advantage thereof.

General Burnside intending to cross the Rappanannock at Fredericksburg, communicated his plan to General Halleck, and relied for the execution in Washington of a simple order, upon that gentleman's promised assistance. Herein he was deceived, and the consequence is the loss of 10,000 men, December 13, at Fredericksburg, which so paralyzed the army of the Potomac that in five weeks it has not stirred.

Thereupon the President Commander issues an order to the army wherein he declares, that the attack on Fredericksburg was no error, and the repulse only an accident. On examination the Commanders of the three grand divisions of the army of the Potomac declare that the attack was an error, and the successful retreat, a military accident to the enemy.

The President Commander's friends thereupon say Burnside nevertheless is the best commander; it is only the fault of the enemy that they did not get whipped. Burnside tenders his resignation : it is not accepted. The President Commander's friends are confident that the Emancipation Proclamation will conquer the rebellion.

Meanwhile we find at the close of the campaign in Virginia and Maryland of 1862, the strong outworks of Richmond transferred to the right bank of the Rappahannock.

January 18th, 1863.   F. A. P.